The

Zen

of Meeting Women

2nd Edition

by Max Weiss

The Zen of Meeting Women

2nd Edition

Visit our website at http://TheZenofMeetingWomen.com

You can email the author at
Max@thezenofmeetingwomen.com

Acknowledgments

I'd sincerely like to thank everyone in the PUA community that has shared their ideas and successes. In particular, a big thanks to Chief for all the helpful comments and suggestions, many of which have found their way into this new edition. Thanks also to everyone that bought the first edition and emailed me with questions and comments.

I'd also like to thank all the wonderful people I've met in the Zen community, and the many teachers who have shared their wisdom in writing. Many of their books are listed in the back of this one. If you want to learn more about Zen, the books I list are a great starting place.

Most of all, I want to thank Mary. As always, this one's for you.

Table of Contents:

Acknowledgments i

Introduction and Frequently Asked Questions..............1

Who this book is for 2
What you will learn.. 3
What's new in the 2nd Edition? 4

Zen 101 ....**5**

What is Zen? 5
The Precepts 7
What's the point?... 11

Meditation **13**

Why meditate?.. 13
How to meditate - Zazen... 15
Problems you might encounter 20
Other types of meditation 21

Non-attachment – don't get obsessed..........................**24**

The problem of attachment 24
How to achieve non-attachment.................................. 25
Be aware of attachment... 26
Zen all day, Zen all night 28

What are your goals? **30**

What do you want?.. 31
Picture what you want... 31
Why do you want that?.. 32

Overview of the Zen of meeting women **37**

Building and growing.. 37
Focus on success... 38

Where and when to meet women 40

Assess the situation 41
Group dynamics and Set Theory 43
Night Game versus Day Game 48
Meeting women online 50
Putting it all together 52

Approaching 53

The death of pickup lines 54
The rise of the canned "opener" 54
The spontaneous opener 56
Once more, with feeling! 57
What are you going to say next? 60

Pump it up! 68

Back to the bookstore 70
Find the emotion, theme, feeling, or trait. Notice,
admire, and relate 75

Turn it up to eleven! 80

Statement of Intent 81
Nonverbal cues – body language 88
The Magic Touch – "Kino" 91

Learning and growing 95

Success versus failure 95

Closing 101

Making plans 101
Instant date 103
Kiss the girl 105

Keeping the ball rolling 107

Talking on the phone 108
Flirting through email and texting 108

The next meeting 109
Why venue change is stressful 111
The *next* next meeting 112
Hey, this is easy! 113

Zen and the art of making love 114

Focus on her 114
Talking about . . . um . . . you know 115
Roadblocks, hurdles, and potholes 116
Basking in the afterglow 117

Relationships - making them last 118

Indra's Net 121
Final words 122

Additional Reading 123

Introduction and Frequently Asked Questions

First things first. What on earth does Zen have to do with meeting women? Zen is all about enlightenment and realizing your enlightened nature. Meeting women is all about, well . . . um . . . what is meeting women all about? It depends on what your goals are. Why do you want to meet women? What will you do once you start meeting them more easily, and feel more comfortable talking to them and hanging out with them. Where will it lead? What path will you take? Perhaps, you'll find that a barrier has been removed, that something was holding you back from being the person you could be. Maybe the negative messages and fears swirling in your brain were holding the true you back from going out and exploring, having fun, and being alive.

In Zen we learn that delusion prevents us from realizing our true nature. Often in meeting women the same is true. You have a lot to offer another person, but you'll never get there if you can't even walk up and say hello. The false assumptions and negative messages you carry could prevent you from doing that.

So The Zen of Meeting Women is first and foremost about removing barriers, opening your eyes to reality, and living in the now. If you do that you will find that you have an easier time meeting women and spending time with them. And you'll also see improvements in other parts of your life. This book focuses on a single application of a process that can be applied to everything. Because it is everything. And so are you.

Who this book is for

Ok, before I get too confusing or mystical or whatever, let's get down to who this book is for. It's for you. How do I know? Well, you're reading this, aren't you? That means you either want to know more about Zen, women, or both. That desire to learn more is all you'll need. I'll do the rest. To a point. There are assignments that you will have to carry out to make progress, but we take baby steps. You may have to push a little outside your comfort zone, but only a little at a time. Once you realize there was nothing to fear, you'll push just a tiny bit farther. And so on. Before you know it, instead of taking baby steps you'll feel like you're sprinting. This process serves two complimentary purposes. First, you'll be making clear and steady progress toward your objectives in meeting great women. Second, that very success will involve what Dr. Paul Dobransky calls "doing courage." In the process of facing and conquering your fears, you will become a better man, the type of man that naturally attracts women. You'll be shedding the delusion that you are doomed to live your life as a wuss, and instead find the attractive, powerful, connected, enlightened person within. So if you want to improve your social skills, meet more women, and learn a bit about Zen along the way, you're in the right place.

What you will learn

This book will take you from start to finish through the process of meeting women, getting to know them, getting to know them better, getting to know them really really well, getting to know them really super really extra . . . ok, you get the point. Anyway, you'll go from that to the process of nurturing a lasting relationship, if that's your thing. If you just end up meeting a lot of great women, that's ok with me. But ultimately, some day, you might find The One. And then it's good to know what happens next, and how to keep from messing up a good thing.

Along the way I'm going to introduce you to many of the fundamental concepts of Zen, and show you how these can help you along the path of meeting women. It can help in a lot of other areas of your life, too. I am not selling a religion here, but if you end up interested in learning more about Zen, go for it. If not, then use the stuff that helps you and toss the rest out. My main objective is to give you a foolproof method for working past the obstacles that stand between you and that beautiful woman you've been dying to meet.

How is this all magically going to happen? Well, it might feel like magic, but behind the scenes you'll be taking very practical and simple steps along the path to meeting women. With each step will come more knowledge and experience. There will be many successes along the way. Before you know it, you'll be walking up to women and starting a conversation with no problem. Don't believe me? Read on. One of the cool things about being a human is that you can learn to do anything. You have access to resources that are greater than any challenge in the world. We're going to tap into those resources and show you what's possible.

This is going to be tons of fun. But before we get to the women, let's start with a very basic foundation in Zen. We'll build on and expand upon this basic understanding as we progress through the rest of the book, so don't skip this part. This is where it all begins.

What's new in the 2nd Edition?

I've gotten a lot of valuable feedback from people who read the first edition of this book, and I've gone through and revised the entire book with that feedback in mind. Some sections are pretty much what they were in the original, with just some stylistic tweaking. Some sections have gotten a major face-lift. And then there is the totally new material. In particular, thanks to the valuable feedback of master pickup artist "Chief" I've added a brief section on "night game" and "set theory". There's also new material on meeting women online. There's a whole lot more, but instead of talking about it, let's just dive right in. Let's not keep the woman of your dreams waiting.

Zen 101

What is Zen?

Zen is a form of Buddhism. Buddhism is based on the teachings of Buddha over 2500 years ago. He taught that there is suffering in life; that suffering has causes, such as anger, craving, greed, ignorance, and attachment; that there is a way to end these causes of suffering; and that way is the Eightfold Path.

Ok, so what's the Eightfold Path? Well, for just 20 monthly payments of $9.99 I'll tell you. Just kidding. It's eight categories of ways to behave or not behave. The categories are Right View, Right Intention, Right Speech, Right Action, Right Livelihood, Right Effort, Right Mindfulness, and Right Concentration. Within each of these are several things to do or not do, but these aren't rules like the 10 Commandments. Rather they are things that one will naturally do when one is enlightened, and that will help bring one to realize enlightenment when they are done. So for example, under the category of Right Action is abstaining from sexual misconduct and keeping sexual relationships with others harmless. It's difficult to realize enlightenment if you're sexually abusing people. Make sense? And by the way, this does not mean you're not allowed to have kinky sex. It means you aren't going to hurt other people emotionally, or force them to do things they haven't agreed to do. Obviously, an enlightened person would already be acting according to this concept. And obviously, someone who consciously acts according to this concept will be moving closer to his natural enlightened state. See how that works? If you want to learn more about the rest of the eightfold path there are many good resources online. I particularly like the one at http://www.thebigview.com/buddhism/eightfoldpath.html .

Ok, so what's all this got to do with meeting women? Easy there, Grasshopper, there's a bit more background you need before we bring it all together. Buddhism started in India, spread to China where it was influenced by Taoism, and then spread to Japan, where Zen Buddhism flourished. Zen Buddhism has a strong emphasis on meditation, as well as person to person transmission of enlightenment. The meditation part we'll get to later. In fact I'm going to teach you how to do Zen meditation, which is called Zazen. As for person to person transmission, the concept here is that you can read all you want about Zen and Buddhism, but to really make progress you need a Zen teacher. Therefore, if you are interested in learning more about Zen, beyond what I can expose you to in a book, you should find out if there is a Zen center near you. The internet is a great resource for this. In the U.S. you can search:

http://directory.google.com/Top/Society/Religion_and
_Spirituality/Buddhism/Lineages/Zen/Centers/United_St
ates/

Ultimately, through meditation and meeting with a teacher you'll work your way toward realizing that you are enlightened. In fact all people are enlightened, it's just we get so lost in our delusions that we need help realizing our own inherent "Buddha Nature."

But even without meditation, even without a teacher, there are those little Zen moments in life. You're sitting watching a sunset, or a river flowing by, or laying back on the grass staring up at the clouds, and you feel like you're a part of it all. Reality is you and the sunset and the river and the clouds, it all just is. And then your cell phone rings and your boss asks where the heck you've been and the whole thing pops like a bubble. You're right back in delusion-ville. Sorry, that's life. While this book is no substitute for working one on one with a Zen teacher, you will learn to meditate, which will inevitably lead to more of those Zen moments popping up in your life. Some of them will involve meeting women. And that's where the fun begins.

The Precepts

One step that many Zen practitioners take along the path to realizing enlightenment is taking the precepts. This means agreeing to a set of guidelines that vary depending on where you are studying Zen. These are not rules that you must follow. Rather, they are ways of behaving that will be natural to you when you are in touch with your true self. Here is a good example of precepts that some Zen practitioners agree to follow:

- I will be mindful of all life, I will not be violent and I will not kill.

- I will respect the property of others, I will not take what is not mine
- I will be conscious and loving in my relationships, I will not give in to lust.
- I will honor honesty and truth, I will not lie.
- I will exercise proper care of my body and mind, I will not be gluttonous nor abuse alcohol or drugs.

All of these are important, and it's worth examining them in a bit more detail as they relate to our goal; meeting women. Let's start with not being violent. I know, it seems pretty common sense that you should not be a violent person, and you definitely should not be violent with women. But apparently it isn't obvious to everyone. If you have problems in this area, put this book down, get the phone book, and call a therapist, psychiatrist, or someone else who can help. Women are very intuitive and if you are approaching them with unresolved issues of this type, they will run the other way. Which in turn will add to your frustration and problems. You need to break the cycle of violence and open your eyes to reality before you can hope to have a positive relationship with anyone.

Respecting the property of others also seems common sense enough. If in your life you are taking something that isn't yours, you need to examine that part of your life. Only by feeling good about yourself will you be able to project a positive image that will attract women. Do what you know is right, and don't rationalize what you know to be wrong. A clear conscience is a powerful thing. Carrying guilt, however deep you bury it, will hinder your progress. You need to be able to look yourself in the mirror and honestly say, "I am a good person," before you will be able to approach a woman and project the truth to her that you are a good person.

Being loving in your relationships is a biggy. If your objective is to have a bunch of one night stands, well, you can still get to know your partner well enough that you feel love towards her. Hopefully you have more ambitious plans in terms of meeting women and building a positive relationship. If so, love is essential. Love means seeing the person for who they are and appreciating the positive qualities of that person. This is an idea we'll be revisiting several times on our journey to meet women. Keep it in mind. As for not giving in to lust, again I have to emphasize, this is not some big prohibition on how you and your lady choose to get it on. If you like dressing up like Darth Vader while she's dressed as Princess Leia, hey, may the Force be with you. Not giving in to lust means not using people. If you're having sex with a woman, you should both be enjoying it. It shouldn't all be about just you.

Honesty is another important one, not just for long-term relationships but for all relationships. This includes letting people see you for who you really are, not putting on a front. There are ways to do this and still put your best foot forward. There's nothing dishonest about brushing your teeth, taking a shower, and smiling, but it sure changes the way people react to you. Be a good person, and you can be honest about who you are and attract people. Strip away those negative things that hide the true you. Allow the truth of your positive self to shine through.

Finally, take care of yourself. If you can't afford to join a gym, you can at least buy some dumbbells, get a book on working out from the library, and get in better shape. There are many good free online resources that can help you get in shape too. One popular on is http://hundredpushups.com . Of course, consult a doctor before embarking on any new exercise program. When you work out, even if it's just three days a week for 15 or 20 minutes, you'll be more healthy, you'll have more energy, you'll feel more in touch with your body, you'll prove to yourself that you have the discipline to accomplish long term goals, and you'll look better. These will all contribute directly to your ability to attract women.

While we're on the subject, let's talk about looks. All of us are self conscious about our looks. Either we think we're too short, too tall, too skinny, too fat, or whatever your particular hang up might be. What you'll find as you start meeting more women is that they tend to judge you more on those things you can control than those things you can't. There's not much you can do if you think your legs are too short, but you can at least put on a clean pair of pants. Remember, you can't change your genes, but you *can* change your jeans. So take care of your body and your looks. Make yourself look presentable before you go out, just in case you meet "The One." Clean clothes that fit and a well-groomed appearance tell the world that you care about yourself. If you don't care about yourself, why would anyone else, including the woman you hope to meet. You need to take care of the things you can control and put your best self forward. This is adds to your attractiveness, not just on the outside, but on the inside. A person who cares for himself is a more attractive person all the way around.

As for drugs and alcohol, if you don't feel the need to use them at all, so much the better. But if you do use either one, moderation is the rule. The last thing I want you to do is start having success meeting women and then let that negative voice in your head convince you it was because you were drunk or wasted. You do not need to be high or drunk to feel confident talking to women. In fact, intoxicants will make it harder for you to access the quick, clever mind that will help you keep a conversation flowing. Being a healthy person will help you attract healthy women for healthy fun. Sounds . . . healthy, doesn't it? Take care of your body and mind, and you will attract more healthy female bodies and minds than you'll know what to do with. Well, actually, I think you'll know what to do with them. Go to the gym, right?

What's the point?

If all this sounds preachy, you've missed the point. What was the point? That if you do what you know is right, you'll feel better about yourself, and other people will pick up on that vibe. This will help you attract women, because it will help you feel like you are a person who deserves to attract women. That all ties in with the concept of Karma. Karma means action. Every action has a reaction. Every cause has an effect. Punch someone and they might punch you back. Hug them and they might hug you back. Show someone what you appreciate about them, and they will start to appreciate you. Allow those parts of yourself that you consider good to blossom, and you will shine in a way that no one can ignore. This is all important stuff. Zen is about finding something you already have inside you and experiencing it fully, realizing a reality that is already there, but gets obscured by delusion. To get to that reality, you need to let go of the attachments and delusions that are holding you back. Once you do, you'll see yourself in a new light. Don't make changes in your life because I'm telling you to. Make changes that you know you want to make, that you know will make you feel better about yourself. It has to come from within. Everything you need is already there. Just get in touch with it. Listen to the positive voices within.

I don't expect you to just change overnight, and I'm not asking you to magically get in touch with yourself without a little kick-start. There is a way to help yourself with this whole process, and that way is meditation. Meditation is like opening a doorway to you. If you meditate daily, everything else in this book will be much easier. If you don't meditate daily, I will hunt you down and shoot you with my Zen bow and arrow kit. Ok, just kidding. Do what you want, but at least give meditation a try. In the next chapter I'll tell you why meditation is so helpful, and how to do it. Then we get to the exciting stuff. Meeting women. Let's go.

Meditation

Meditation is easy and has many benefits. In this chapter I'm going to discuss why meditation is so great, how it can help in your quest to meet women, and how to do it. And then, you're going to meditate. Really.

Why meditate?

We live in a stressful world, and that stress gets even higher when we are approaching women we want to meet. This is called approach anxiety, and it is common. It's ok to get a little stressed out, but you don't want it to prevent you from making the approach, or cause you to blow it once you make the approach. While I'm not suggesting you should plop yourself down in the lotus position before the woman of your dreams, I am suggesting that you can find that place of inner peace more easily once you've spent some quality time there.

Meditation is a great way to relax and deal with stress. It's also a great way to get in touch with yourself and the reality that we're all a part of. We tend to live our lives in patterns, playing the same programs over and over. Get up, eat cereal, brush teeth, get on train, go to work, and so on. It's possible to find a richness in every task, every moment. Meditation helps show you the way to that inner richness. It gives you a place from which to observe yourself without all the usual programs playing. Unpeel the layers of delusion and you'll find something amazing inside, something that was always there, but you weren't paying attention to.

Meditation helps you learn how to notice. Notice what? Everything. Stop and smell the roses, see the green grass and the blue sky. Pay attention to everything around you. These skills will directly help you when you're talking to a woman. Learn to listen when people are talking instead of just planning out the next thing you want to say. Get into the flow of the conversation, instead of being stuck in "I talk, you talk." Notice the way she's standing, what she's doing with her hands, the way she's looking at you, and still pay close attention to what she's saying. Sound difficult? Not if you are in the moment, just being there with her, being completely aware. Meditation gives you a taste of this being in the moment stuff. And it does so in a safe environment, away from the daily stress of life. Once you experience this, you can bring it to other aspects of your life, including your conversations and interactions with women.

You'll also learn to be aware of your own thoughts. Are some of these thoughts negative messages that have been holding you back? Maybe it's time to replace them with positive thoughts. That's not some New Age mumbo jumbo; the power of positive thinking is real and you can use it to improve your self-image and the way others see you. Who would you rather talk to, someone who perceives himself as boring or someone who feels alive and interesting? Would you rather hang out with someone who brings you up or someone that brings you down? The key is not to block out or ignore negative messages. Rather, you can confront them, examine them, spin them around, and send them drifting off. Realize them for what they are, just ideas. If you think you're too fat, that's not necessarily a negative thought. If you focus on the thought and feel depressed and eat a bucket of ice cream, well, that's not so good. If you think up ways to lose some weight and become healthier, then that is good. So being aware of what's going on in your head, and examining those thoughts, is an important process. Don't cling or attach to those thoughts. See them for what they are, and move on. Find what's helpful and learn from it. Discard what's harmful and holding you back. Look for positive solutions to the problems you face, and act on those solutions.

There are many more benefits to meditation, but for our purposes the main idea is this. You need to become more aware of yourself and the world around you in order to interact more effectively and live more comfortably in that world. You and the world aren't two separate things, it's all one thing. Feeling that, knowing that, comes from meditation, and the benefits that result will directly help your efforts to meet wonderful women and develop relationships with them. We'll revisit these ideas and flesh them out as the book progresses, but you need to be meditating or you'll miss a lot. So let's get you meditating.

How to meditate - Zazen

Meditation is very easy, and the more you do it, the easier it gets. I suggest you start out meditating 5 minutes a day, every day. Then increase that to 10 minutes, and so on, till you get to about 30 or 40 minutes a day. If that's too much, do it for less time, but do it every day. You'll realize the best results that way. Better you should meditate 5 minutes a day, every day, than 40 minutes every other day. Make this a natural part of your life, just like taking a shower in the morning. Here's what you need to do:

Sit in a comfortable stable position

You don't have to sit in a full lotus position, although if you can, that's a very stable position to sit in. If you choose to do a full lotus, use a thick pillow to sit on so your butt is higher than your knees, and your knees are on the floor. There are other positions you can use on the floor such as half lotus and Burmese. To learn more, take a look at the pictures at:

http://www.mro.org/zmm/teachings/meditation.php

If you don't want to sit on the floor, sit on a chair. You still might want the pillow; it can help get you in a comfortable position. Sit slightly forward on the chair, and don't lean back against the backrest.

The important thing is to find a stable sitting position that won't have you squirming around and fidgeting. You need to sit still and breathe, so find a position that allows that.

Head tilted slightly down

Your head should be facing forward and tilted slightly down. This should feel comfortable and natural. If your head is tilted so far down that it's interfering with your breathing, you're tilting too much.

Eyes almost closed

Your eyes should be almost but not quite shut. Look at a spot on the floor a few feet in front of you. This should feel comfortable, not strained. Your eyes should be relaxed.

Hands in cosmic mudra

Your hands should be resting in your lap, right hand first with the palm up, then left hand on top, of the right, palm up. Your thumbs should be close but not quite touching, with enough space to just pass a sheet of paper between them. This hand position is called the cosmic mudra. There are other mudras, but this one is good for our purposes. It also has the coolest name.

One way to check if you've got your mind on your meditation is to check the thumbs. If they are pressed together or are far apart, get them back in the right spot, almost touching, and continue.

Back upright and comfortable

Your back should be upright, but don't strain to make it perfectly straight or arched. Just sit up in a comfortable position. This might take some practice. Before you start meditating, you can rock from side to side till you find the mid point. Then rock forward and back in ever decreasing arcs to find the balance point in the middle. Don't slump forward as this will affect your breathing.

Don't tighten the back muscles as this will get painful fast. Over time this will become easier. In the beginning it will take a bit of trial and error. It's all part of the process, so don't let it stress you out. You are learning. Just pay attention and stay open to what's happening.

Breathe down to your belly

Many of us get in the bad habit of breathing into our chest rather than all the way down to our belly. Your stomach should gently rise and fall as you breathe. Don't try to slow down your breathing, just breathe at a comfortable rate and be aware of your breathing. You can focus either on the feeling of the air going in and out of your nose, or the feeling of the air making your belly rise and fall. As your meditation continues your breathing will naturally slow down. That's fine. Don't try to control it, just be aware of it. How does it feel? Your breath is always with you, so it's a nice thing to focus on. All living things are breathing with you, even the trees and the grass. The universe is breathing. It's a universal meditation that's going on all the time, and you're tapping into it, plugging back in.

Mind aware of thoughts

Your mind will do its normal thing, which is to think think think. You will get distracted, and ride off on this tangent and that. That's going to happen. Once you become aware of it, gently bring your mind back to your breathing. Ultimately, you will be able to see your thoughts floating by like clouds, rather than getting wrapped up in them and carried off. This takes time and is a process of constant improvement. Don't worry if you keep getting distracted. Just come back to the breathing. Again, don't let any of this stress you out. From the very first moment you sit to meditate, you are doing it right, and will continue to improve.

Count your breaths

One way to keep your mind focused on your breathing is to count each breath. At first, you can count up from 1 to 10, counting each in and each out breath. Then start over at 1. This is harder than it sounds, but will become easier. Your mind will tend to drift. Just bring it back to the counting.

When that becomes easy, which could take weeks or months, start counting just the out breaths, 1 to 10, 1 to 10, on and on. Really focus on each number as you say it or think it silently in your head.

Breathe in, then out: ooooonnnnneeee.

Breathe in, then out: twooooooooooooo.

And so on. If you lose the count, and you will from time to time, start over at 1. This is not a contest, it is a process. It becomes easier with practice, and you'll find it another great way to monitor how well you're focusing on your breathing rather than getting lost in thoughts.

Eventually, you might want to stop counting, but some people continue this for years. This is still real meditation, even if you do the counting. Sometimes you will notice what's happening between the numbers. This might be a calm feeling, or it might be a deep feeling that has no name. Just notice it all. Let it all be part of your experience. There is no right or wrong here. Just let it be.

Problems you might encounter

Feeling uncomfortable

At first, just sitting still for this long will be hard. Your body wants to move around. But only by quieting the body can you quiet the mind. Sit very still, and focus on your breathing and your counting. Stay with it. This does get easier, but only if you stick with it.

Itching

If you feel an itch, focus on it. What does it feel like? What is an itch? Don't try to make it go away, just let your mind focus on it. Don't scratch. If you scratch one itch, another pops up somewhere else, and so on. Just let it go. This is very hard to do. It's also great training for focusing the mind and staying in the moment. You can be aware of what's happening without it controlling you. Right? Keep at it. If the itch is really driving you nuts, go ahead and scratch, but don't let it turn into a scratching fest. Take a deep breath and get back to focusing on your breathing.

Lost in thoughts

This is the biggy, and although I've already mentioned it, I want to emphasize that your brain just isn't going to shut up. What it will do, eventually, is calm down. Rather than hurling 50 ideas per second at you, it might just be an occasional thought, floating by. You can be aware of that thought, consider it, and let it go. Effortlessly. This takes time. Meditate every day and you will see progress. If you find yourself getting lost in thoughts, do not get angry at yourself or scold yourself. This is part of the process. You're human. Humans think a lot. You'll be amazed how much thinking your brain does. It's really something. Let it do it's thing, you do your thing, and it will all work out.

Other types of meditation

There are many types of meditation, perhaps thousands. I'm teaching you one. It's all you'll ever need. If you want to try other kinds, be my guest. I would warn, however, that if you are under active psychiatric care, you should consult with your psychiatrist before getting into meditation. The type of meditation I'm teaching you is called Zazen, and if you go to a Zen temple this is the type of meditation you'll see people doing. Eventually, you can leave off the number counting and just sit. Or you can focus on solving a koan, which is a sort of Zen riddle. Here's an example of one:

"Huìnéng asked Hui Ming, 'Without thinking of good or evil, show me your original face before your mother and father were born'."

If any of this interests you, I want to remind you, life is short. Don't wait for "some day" to seek out a Zen teacher. Do it today and learn more. It's a great way to meet people. And meeting people is a good way to work on the social skills that you'll be using as we progress through this book.

See how it all connects? Start noticing that more in your life. The universe is one big connected happening and we're all part of it. Just a big stew of atoms floating around. If you don't want to study Zen, study physics and astronomy. It's practically the same thing.

Whoops, see how my mind got lost on a tangent. Weird. Let's get back to business. While we're on the subject of meditation, I want to briefly tell you about another type of meditation that might interest you, and then I'm going to give you your first assignment.

Mindfulness meditation is being aware or "mindful" of stuff. What stuff? You know . . . stuff! Trees, birds, grass, sky, table, the taste of your food, how it feels to walk, how the wind sounds rustling the leaves. Be aware of the present moment. As with Zazen, you'll notice that the mind likes to chitter chatter. You can see those thoughts for what they are without comment or judgment, and then let them go. You can be mindful while walking around the block, or strumming a guitar, or doing the dishes. Feel free to experiment with focusing on something in your immediate surroundings and staying present in this moment, it can be very relaxing. But that's not the assignment. That's extra credit. The assignment is as follows.

First of all, I want you to start meditating every day. Give it a try. Come on, humor me. You have nothing to lose

> **Assignment # 1**
> **Meditate every day, even if it's just for 5 minutes. Try it, you'll like it.**

and so much to gain. Do Zazen meditation as described in this chapter every day for at least 5 minutes.

Second of all, for one whole day I want you to focus on people. People you pass on the sidewalk, people you interact with, people you see driving by. What do they look like? How do they stand, walk, sit? What do they tell you with their body language, with their posture, with their expression and tone of voice? Could they change any of these things if they wanted to? Would it change your reaction to them? Can you change these things about yourself? How is your posture, expression, tone of voice? Can you consciously change them? For how long? What are your "default" settings? Pay attention to this stuff and think about it. This is important stuff. We communicate an awful lot to each other without even opening our mouths.

Humans are very perceptive. Tap into that and see what you learn from the process. You might want to carry a notebook and write down your observations. You might make this a daily habit.

Assignment # 2
Notice people, how
they act, move, look.
How does this affect
you? What does it
communicate?

One more thing. If you happen to see a woman you like, notice what it is about her that caught your eye. Her hair? Her smile? Her body? The way she moves? Her energy? Was she laughing? What attracted you? Why? Did you manage to catch her eye? How did that feel? Was there a little charge of electricity? Fear? Excitement? Be aware of this stuff. You aren't trying to change your natural reactions. Just become aware of them.

In summary then, be aware.

Now.

Non-attachment – don't get obsessed

Have you ever met a woman, and then thought about her all day. And all the next day. And all the next week. And then when you bump into her the next time, you're tongue tied and nervous. Why? Because you're letting yourself get obsessed. In this chapter we're going to learn how to break that pattern. It isn't helping, so let's put an end to it once and for all.

The problem of attachment

In Zen Buddhism there is the concept of attachment. Attachment is an exaggerated desire to possess something or be with someone. It is an unmindful clinging. Excessive desire shifts our focus to the object of that desire, and away from everything else. It isn't balanced.

Attachment is a root cause of our suffering. We desire an expensive new car. If we get that car, does our suffering end? Or do we move on to the next attachment? Attachment enslaves us.

Non-attachment ends our enslavement; it frees us. Non-attachment means we can live in the world and observe the things around us without craving and lusting after them. It does not mean shutting off emotion. It means living in balance, being part of the world and not getting stuck on this thing or that thing, this person or that person. I'm not talking about apathy, you still care. This is about being aware and alive and flowing, not stuck, trapped, and obsessed.

How to achieve non-attachment

So how do we rid ourselves of attachment? It ain't easy. Especially living in a society where everything is for sale and we are constantly bombarded by advertisements designed to create desire and attachment. It's tough to ignore all the radio jingles, TV commercials, billboards, magazine ads, internet ads, etc. It's all around us every day. On top of that, even if you weren't surrounded by messages meant to increase desire, the human ego itself is a constant craving machine. Our ego keeps us from realizing enlightenment.

Let go of attachments. Let go of greed. Let go of the ego. How? Daily meditation is very helpful. It enables you to notice when you are acting out of greed or attachment, and to also feel what it's like to just be, without attachment. Meditation is enlightenment. If you haven't started meditating on a daily basis, go back to the last chapter, read it, and practice it. Meditation isn't just about reducing stress, although it's certainly good for that. It's about seeing reality, being in reality. It gives you the perspective to see the ways in which you might be acting out of attachment, and what the results of those actions are. It helps you to let go of attachment and just live.

So how do we apply this to the situation with the woman you're obsessing over? You meet her, and you have a crush, a craving, a lust. You can't get her out of your head. What to do? Should you run off and meditate till she disappears? Nope, that's not what I'm suggesting. This is an opportunity for you to realize something important. Part of that obsession comes from a **scarcity mindset**. It triggers little voices in your head. "She talked to me. That's it. If I blow it with her, who knows when I'll talk to such a great woman. If I fail with her it will be a catastrophe. I can not fail, or else. Everything is riding on this. Must . . . not . . .fail!"

Bam! Too late, you already failed. By feeding your brain this type of stuff, you practically guarantee that you will blow it the next time you encounter her. You've practically been rehearsing failure. Desperation will be writ large, and this will push her away. Neediness is your enemy. It turns people off. You must change that scarcity mindset to an **abundance mindset**. Part of that will come from successfully approaching and talking to many women, which we will get to later. I promise. But it's a bit of a "Catch 22." To approach the women successfully, you need to get rid of the scarcity mindset, but to get rid of it, you need to have approached a bunch of women successfully. Don't worry. That's why we are taking baby steps into this process. Your skills will grow right alongside your abundance mindset. It will all happen together. Organically and naturally.

Be aware of attachment

For now, however, we need to lay some groundwork. Step one is noticing when you are acting out of attachment, obsession, neediness, or a scarcity mindset. So that's the next assignment. Again, you might want to keep a journal, but ultimately this is more of a "noticing things in the moment" kind of assignment. If writing it down helps, great. If not, don't worry. Either way, focus your energy on noticing when you are acting out of attachment, or thinking in terms of neediness or scarcity. Of course, you should also note those times when you are acting out of an abundance mindset. Even simple things count. Let's say you go to the big warehouse grocery store and there are hundreds of bright red apples piled up. Do you feel panicky? Probably not, unless you need every apple sitting there and then some. More likely you feel like you can just take your time and grab a few

> **Assignment # 3**
> **Notice when you are**
> **acting out of a**
> **scarcity mindset, and**
> **notice when you are**
> **acting out of an**
> **abundance mindset.**

apples. If other people come up and start looking at the apples, no big deal. There are enough for everyone. How does that feel? You can actually just relax and pick out some apples. No stress, no attachment. That is exactly how you want to feel when talking to a woman. There are other women. This one might be right for me, or she might not. I don't know. I'll talk to her and find out. And if there's a mutual attraction, things will probably work out. If not, then that's ok too. It's more experience talking to women, and that's always a good thing. I'll just go talk to the next woman. And so on.

Do you see how that could be liberating? Do you see how something so simple as a change of perspective could make a really powerful change in the way you relate to and interact with women? And that new way of relating to and interacting women might bring more success. Do you see how the broader perspective that comes with daily meditation might be helpful to you in trying to change your mindset and get a new perspective? If not, then sit a few days. Yes, there will be a lot of drifting off lost in thought. But occasionally you'll really just be present, just in the moment, breathing and counting. In that peaceful moment, what do you lack? What is missing? You don't need to crave anything, because you are already everything. It's all here, right now. If you can take just a little tiny piece of that with you throughout the day, if you can feel that reality there with you as you interact with people, it will slowly change the way you interact. You will open up, and the world will open up. I'm not suggesting that any of this is easy. But it isn't hard either. You can make it happen through persistence and awareness. Small incremental progress each day will eventually add up to a mountain of success. You have everything you need within you right now. Take the first step, then the next, then the next, and remember to enjoy the journey along the way.

Zen all day, Zen all night

But hey, you can't just meditate all day, what are you supposed to do the rest of the day? Well, that's where the eightfold path and the precepts come in handy. If you don't know what the heck I'm talking about, go back to Zen 101. Start incorporating this stuff into your life. In particular, if you haven't started some sort of exercise program, I strongly encourage you to do so. It's worth it just for the extra energy it gives you, and you'll look and feel better every day. Tune up your mind with meditation. Tune up your body with exercise. You're unstoppable! And don't forget about the mindfulness meditation I mentioned last chapter, and the observations from the second assignment. Feel free to continue observing and being aware in your daily life. It all counts and it all moves you toward achieving your goals. Develop these good habits and success will happen.

But how do we define success? What are your goals? Next we need to ask these basic questions so you can better focus your efforts in the chapters that follow. You need to know where you're going if you ever hope to get there. Then we'll look at an overview of the Zen of meeting women, and then we dive into the process itself. So let's look at your goals, then figure out how to achieve them.

What are your goals?

Ok, you want to meet women. Why? What's the objective? A friend, girlfriend, someone to have sex with, someone to go see a movie with, someone to show your comic book collection to, someone to marry? Think this over and dig down. What is it that you hope to achieve? Once you decide what you want, the next step is to ask why you want that. What will it give you? Why is that important to you? These might seem like silly questions, but if you really ask them deeply and take the time to answer them, everything I'm going to teach you about how to meet women will make more sense. You'll know why you're doing this. You'll know what your motivation is. And this will keep you from stopping halfway through the process. If you keep your eyes on the prize, you'll have an easier time getting it. That doesn't mean, by the way, that you attach to your goal and obsess over it. Rather, it gives you a direction to travel in. With each step you move closer to your goal, but each step itself is a part of the journey and should be appreciated. Live your life now, not in some imagined future.

What do you want?

So let's break this down. What is your objective? If you really follow through with the Zen of meeting women, you are going to meet a lot of women. A lot. You'll have lots of conversations, get lots of phone numbers and email addresses, and have the opportunity to continue from there. But that is not an end in itself. Some of these women might become friends, some will become more than just friends. How many girlfriends do you really want or need? Remember, while you want abundance to chase away the scarcity mindset, you don't want every hour of every day devoted to hanging out with women. A little moderation might be advisable. Do you want one girlfriend? More than one? How about one main one, with a group of prospects waiting in the wings? As long as you're honest with everyone about what your relationship is, it's really up to you to decide. Not ready for marriage? That's fine. Looking for a wife? That's fine. It's all up to you. The important thing is you keep the goal in mind and let that goal guide your actions. If you've met the woman of your dreams and have been dating her for months and months, keeping twenty other girlfriends hanging on might not be such a good idea. Decide what you want, and do what feels right to you. Just keep moving toward your goal.

Picture what you want

Take a moment now, put the book down (after you read this section), and picture in your mind what the ideal outcome of this process will be for you. Going out every night with a different woman, or sitting on the couch watching a movie with one special one.

Whatever it is, I want you to picture it clearly. I can't do this part for you, it's up to you to decide what you really want and picture it clearly in your mind. And remember, the question here is what do you want. If some nagging voice comes flying in from nowhere saying, "what? That will never happen," just send that voice packing. It won't happen if you don't let it

happen. Open up, and let yourself dream. What is your ideal outcome? Put the book down now and don't pick it back up till you've done this.

**Assignment # 4
Picture your ideal outcome.**

Ok, did you do it? What? You didn't? Hey, look. This is the easy stuff. We are taking baby steps. But if you don't take them, you are not going to learn to run. Really, do this. Take a deep breath, close your eyes, and picture your ideal outcome. Don't worry, I'll still be here when you get back.

There we go! Ok, hopefully whatever it is you just pictured is actually legal. If not, go back and revise. And remember precept #3, "I will be conscious and loving in my relationships." If the picture doesn't include being loving, I think that is likewise cause for revision. Love can be brief, but without it, you'll find this a meaningless exercise. We are not out to feed the insatiable ego, we are out to slay it.

Why do you want that?

Now that we have a goal, we can move to the next step. Let's examine *why* you want whatever it is you decided you want. Let's say your image is of you walking hand in hand with a beautiful woman. Nice and romantic.

It's a spring day. Birds are chirping. The sun is shining. The stock market is up. Everything is perfect. Ok, so why do you want that? What will it give you? If the answer is, it will boost my ego, we have some work to do. While it's true that being in a loving relationship will make you feel better, it's because you are sharing your life with another person. You have someone special to experience the spring day with. It isn't about your ego, it's about living life even more fully. It's about being with someone that sees something special in you, not just someone that gives you something. Remember, we are trying to avoid coming from a place of neediness. If you walk up to a woman and say, "hey, will you go out with me? My ego could really use a boost," what would you expect her to say? If you're lucky, she'll take it as a joke. If not, she's likely to think you're nuts. Now what if you walk up to the same woman and say, "hey, you look like someone I'd like to know better. Let's spend some time together and see if we have something to share." My guess is you'd at least get her interest. But we aren't going to say that out loud. We're going to come from a place inside that speaks those words through our actions, our body language, our expression, our very being. If you just say the words, she might not believe them. If you live the words, if you embody them, then there will be no convincing to do. It will be truth, and she will pick up on that truth the more she is with you. That's powerful stuff.

So back to our question, why do you want the outcome you've pictured? What will it do, what will it mean, why is it important? You need to answer these very important questions for yourself. So let's do that right now, while we're on a roll. Set down the book again—and I do hope you're setting it down in a nice clean spot—and picture your ideal outcome again.

Then ask yourself, "what will I have if I make this come true, why is this important to me?" Do it now.

Ok, that was actually a tough one. I should have warned you. Sorry about that. Oh well. You may not have come up with The Definitive Answer, but hopefully it got you thinking about what it is you really want and why. Feel free to come back to this from time to time. Your answer might change, and that's fine. We aren't attaching to one answer or one reason, or even one ideal outcome. All of this stuff can change over time. The point is to have an idea of what you want now, and to work on that now. If it changes later, well, you'll deal with that later. That's life. All you have to do is work on the present, and let the "future you" worry about the future. Sound good?

And by the way, you might find your mind drifting back to your ideal image and your reason for wanting it during meditation. That's fine, let it. Spend a little time drifting around there, and then after you've chewed it over, get back to counting your breaths. Sometimes during meditation important stuff comes up, and it's ok to deal with that stuff before you get back to meditating. It's all part of the process.

One more thing I should toss in here. It can be helpful to ask yourself not only what you want and why you want it, but also, how will you know when you get it. Sometimes this is obvious. If want you want is to be married, then when you're standing up there taking your vows, it will be quite clear that you achieved your goal. But if what you want is a little more loosey goosey, like "I want a loving relationship with someone I respect and am attracted to," that's a little tougher. So ask yourself, how will I know when I've achieved my goal. What will that look like, sound like, feel like. Although we don't want to obsess with achieving any one specific goal, it's important to recognize when you're making progress toward a goal and when you've achieved a goal. If you achieve a goal, it's a good time to celebrate, and to set a new goal, so that you're always growing, living, and learning.

So you know what you want and why you want it. You know what it will be like when you get it. You've started exercising and meditating. You've done all the assignments so far, and you're starting to notice the way people communicate things about themselves nonverbally. You notice your own nonverbal communication, and you are working to improve from the inside out and the outside in.

You have also become aware of those times you are acting out of a scarcity mindset rather than an abundance mindset. You are letting go of attachment, letting yourself feel what it's like to not obsess over this and that. It's all starting to make a little bit of sense, somehow.

Now it's time to get the roadmap for the rest of the process, then fill our tank and go. Don't worry, we're still taking baby steps every bit of the way. Nothing up ahead is any more difficult than what we've already done. It's just that at a certain point you're going to realize the baby grew up and is driving a lean, mean, attraction machine. Do every assignment, continue with your daily meditation, and you will get there.

Overview of the Zen of meeting women

The Zen of meeting women is going to be broken down into the following steps. We will discuss where to go to meet women, how to approach them, what to say, dealing with nervousness, how to keep the conversation flowing, and building attraction through touch and the right words. We'll talk about "night game" and take a detour to the virtual world of the internet. After that, we'll discuss sex and long-term relationships. Then you get your Zen of meeting women medallion, to wear proudly wherever you go. Well, feel free to make the medallion yourself, but I'd keep it hidden. What you actually get is the ability to walk up to a woman you've never met before, and connect with her very quickly. Remember, with great power comes great responsibility. You are going to be responsible with this stuff, right? Review the precepts, then get back here and we'll see how this process is going to unfold.

Building and growing

Each of these steps is going to be broken down further. We'll also revisit some of these ideas from time to time as we move along. If you haven't figured this out yet, I'd like to mention that we are building something amazing here. This is a process through which your skills grow, and that only happens if you keep everything happening all together, adding new skills as we go, continuing to practice the old skills throughout the process. All of this will eventually become very natural, but it's going to take practice. It's also going to take persistence.

This is a learning process, and as we learn we can sometimes make mistakes. A mistake is a learning opportunity, not a failure. You learn, revise, and try again. Each time you're a little better, a little more confident, and everything will come together a little easier. If negative stuff comes up from your past, it's coming up for a reason. So you can learn from it, and then let it go. If positive stuff comes up from your past, it's to remind you that you can succeed. It's all good, and it's all part of the process. Just keep building and growing. Remember, the only failure is not trying. If you try, you will learn and grow. It's a natural process.

Focus on success

So that's it for the overview, but before we dive in I have another exercise. You can put this one off till later if you're anxious to get started, but please do it at some point. I want you to think about all the successes you've had in your relationships. These relationships can be familial, romantic, business, or friendships. The point is to bring up

---

Assignment # 6
Recall your successful relationships, and realize that you deserve to have more.

---

the positive feelings associated with those relationships. You need to realize deep inside that you are a good person, and you deserve to have successful and positive relationships with people. You have something unique to offer. And that makes you attractive. Anytime you're dealing with approach anxiety or having trouble with any step in the process, revisit these memories and feelings. The mind is a powerful thing, and you can harness that power to help you achieve your goals. Or you can wallow in self-pity. The choice truly is yours. So try focusing on success and see how that makes you feel. Grab on to that feeling and get ready, you're going to be encountering it a lot more in the future.

Now let's get started!

Where and when to meet women

If we're going to meet women, we need to go where they are. Sound simple? Of course, but there's more to it than that. Where you meet a woman and what she's doing when you first encounter her is going to affect our approach. So it's worth thinking this through. The variables we need to consider when approaching a woman are:

- Where is she?
- Why is she here?
- Is she busy?
- Is she bored?
- Is she sitting, standing, walking, running?
- What time of day is it?
- Is she in a situation where she'll feel safe if approached by a stranger?
- Is she alone or with friends?

That's a lot to keep in mind, so that's why we're going over it now. Then you can keep it all in the back of your mind without getting stuck analyzing it all the time. We'll have more important things to think about during the approach. So let's do the brainwork now, absorb it all, and move on.

Assess the situation

Where is she and why is she here?

There are lots of places you already go in your day-to-day life. Make a list of the ones that have lots of women. There are other places you don't currently go, but could. Which of those would be good places to meet women? The mall, bar, gym, park, museum, dance class, and cooking class are all possibilities. Think about indoor spaces and outdoor spaces. Where are you more comfortable? Why are you there? Why is she there? If it's a cooking class, for example, you won't feel the pressure to explain your presence, and you'll automatically have an excuse to talk, and something to talk about. That's pretty ideal. You'll also know that you share an interest. Sounds pretty good, right? Contrast that with walking up to the hot babe at the ATM machine. She's probably not interested in talking at the moment, and your approach is likely to make her nervous. Not good.

Where you meet a woman and the reason she is there are important considerations. People go to bars to be social, to the gym to work out, and to the museum . . . well, that could be a mix of wanting to see art and hoping Mr. Right will magically appear. Sometimes you know, sometimes you can guess, and sometimes it's completely up in the air. The point is you need to assess the situation you are already in, and think up situations you could be in that might increase your odds of success.

Is she busy or bored?

The woman at the ATM is busy. The woman drifting through the museum might be bored; you'll have to read her body language for that one. The woman just sitting on the train with nothing to read staring off into space is almost definitely bored. Which one is more likely to welcome a conversation? Start thinking about these things, they make a huge difference. Granted, you might be wrong. The woman at the bookstore with her nose buried in a book might be bored out of her mind. The woman at the ATM machine might be fantasizing about having wild sex with a stranger. The point is not necessarily to rule out an approach, it's to look for the easier, more natural approach. Again, we are looking to increase the odds of success.

Is she sitting, standing, walking, doing cartwheels, running away from you, running towards you?

It's pretty tough to approach a jogger, even if you're jogging too. It's pretty easy to go talk to a woman that's slowly walking down the aisle at a bookstore browsing. There's a different dynamic depending on what she's doing. If she's at the ATM machine, let her finish up and walk away before introducing yourself. If she's sitting on the train with nothing to do, don't wait till she gets up and leaves to come up with the perfect opening line. How long is she likely to stay where she is? How long have you got? Be sensitive to the situation. Be aware.

What time of day is it, and will she be comfortable talking to a stranger?

If it's late at night and she's walking down an unlit street, that is not a good time to approach, unless you like the taste of hot pepper spray. If it's late at night and she's sitting by herself at a bar, that's a different story. Daytime on the same street might be fine. Once again, it's about being aware of what's going on around you, and thinking it through. Don't get bogged down in this, just make a quick assessment of the vibe. If you think the woman would feel threatened or scared if you approach, don't. Otherwise, go ahead and see how it goes.

Group dynamics and Set Theory

Is she alone or with friends?

You might think that if she is with friends it's a bad time to approach. Actually, this might be a more comfortable situation from her perspective than if she's alone. She has her friends around her, so she doesn't have to worry about strangers approaching. If you can charm them all and join the group, great. If she sees that you get along with her friends, she's more likely to warm up to you as well.

Negging and "Cocky and Funny"

There are some who advise virtually ignoring the woman you want to meet while chatting up her friends. You then refer to her with teasing comments, like, "why do you bring her along, she's a handful." In the pickup artist community this is called "negging," and means

43

making joking negative comments. This actually can be very effective, but I'm going to suggest you not do it. A more straightforward approach can be just as effective, and will probably feel better. Anytime you feel you are being manipulative, you're likely to have second thoughts about what you're doing. This will break the flow of the interaction, and discourage you from trying in the future. Just go up and interact with the group, and follow the steps with the woman of your choice that will be discussed later. Keep the whole group engaged, but let her know she is the focus of your attention.

If you do want to try "negging," make sure it's done in a playful manner. The point isn't to insult her or put her down. The point is to have fun and show that you're not scared to interact in a playful way.

Another version of the same concept is what's called "cocky and funny." This method, made famous by David DeAngelo, involves acting both—yes, you guessed it—cocky and funny. Cocky without the funny is just obnoxious. Too much funny without the cocky turns into you entertaining her, like a clown. And as DeAngelo likes to point out, clowns don't get laid. Not often anyway. The cocky and funny style is similar to treating her like your bratty little sister who you love but gets on your nerves. If any of this sounds intriguing, I suggest you look up David DeAngelo on the internet. Or just Google "cocky and funny" and see what you find. The power of this approach is it keeps her guessing. Are you hitting on her or not? Are you interested in her or not? Maybe you're just a really sociable guy who talks to and jokes around with everyone. It's disarming and it's fun, if done correctly.

So why don't I teach cocky and funny in this book? Not everyone is good at acting cocky and funny, and they end up trying to be something they're really not. The style I'm teaching involves what I'll reluctantly call a more natural approach. I'm reluctant to call it that because it sounds like a value judgment, which I don't mean it to be. It's the approach I prefer and one that I think will work for more people, but that doesn't mean you have to agree with me. Some people are naturals when it comes to acting cocky and funny, others just aren't cut out for it. See what works for you. If the Zen approach works, great. If you want to try something like "negging" or cocky and funny, go for it. Mix and match. Take what works and discard the rest. Use what feels congruent with who you really are. If you really are a cocky and funny kind of guy, then use that part of your personality. Just remember to keep it fun rather than insulting. There is no one best style to use for meeting women that will apply equally to all men. There are many styles out there. The ones that feel right to you probably *are* right for you.

Set Theory

Back to the topic at hand, we were discussing whether she's alone or with friends. In the pickup artist community this is referred to as a set. Two women together is a 2-set. Three is a 3-set. Can you guess what four women together is called? The reason this is important is that the bigger the group, the more intimidating it can be to approach. But the bigger the group, the *easier* it can be to achieve success. Crazy, right? But it's true more often than not. That's because the bigger the group is, the scarier it is to everyone. So they are being approached much less than that attractive woman sitting by herself at the bar, who is being approached every two seconds.

In set theory, you approach the group and initially ignore the woman that you're interested in, while focusing on everyone else. You might "neg" her from time to time, saying things like, "is she always like this?" You have to win over the group before you focus on the woman you're interested in. Then you build attraction and comfort with her, and get into "kino", all concepts we'll be discussing later.

So that's set theory in a nutshell. There's more to it, some of which drifts into territory I'd rather not explore. In particular, some men will approach a woman and if he decides he isn't into her, will use her as a "pawn". This means he'll approach a group with her on his arm as a means of instant validation. Obviously, I don't condone using people this way. Learn to approach without using or hurting other people. You'll feel better about yourself and become a more attractive person to others.

The point to take away from all this is you need to be aware that there is a different dynamic if she's alone, with one friend, or with many, and you need to be attuned to that. You can succeed in any of these situations without using "negs" and without using a "pawn". Use the techniques I'm going to teach you in the chapters ahead. If there are other people with the woman you are interested in, definitely connect with them too and make them your friends before focusing your attention on the woman you like. You don't need to "neg" her for this to work. Just be a naturally social person to the whole group before you make your intentions more obvious.

The Wingman

We should also discuss whether you're alone or with friends. Approaching women with a friend has its advantages, especially if she's with friends. Your friend can act as your "wingman" and keep her friends busy while you focus your attention on the woman you really like. But if there's just one woman, approaching with your friend might be a bit odd. Depends on your friend. If he understands his role, he can help. But if he's hitting on the woman you're interested in, that is not good. Or if he's insulting you, that's not good either. A good wingman only says positive things about you, and you about him. You build each other up. He does your bragging for you.

If you have a friend who is interested in meeting new women with you, take him along and see how he does. Is he a help or a hindrance? I'd suggest having him read this book first so you're both "on the same page." Yes, not only did I just make a bad pun, but I put it in quotes to make sure you didn't miss it. I am truly shameless. Let's move on.

If you prefer to go it alone, that's fine. Ultimately you are going to have to talk to this woman by yourself, so don't use a friend as a crutch. Do what works, but don't become dependant on having a friend come along. If you're alone and you see someone you want to meet, go for it. The worst that can happen is you learn more and develop your skills more. That's not too bad when you think about it.

Night Game versus Day Game

Day Game generally means meeting women wherever you happen to be during the day, or going to places you hope to meet women during the day. Most of the examples in this book focus on day game. Why? Because most of us have jobs or school, and see beautiful women we'd like to meet during the day. That's valuable time for practicing and learning, and hopefully meeting great women.

That said, some guys just feel more comfortable practicing in bars and clubs. Going out at night to meet women is Night Game. Pretty much everything in this book applies equally well to Night Game, but there are a few additional considerations. First, most clubs and bars are noisy. It might be harder to have a conversation. Having a deep connected conversation can be even harder still. Bars and clubs are an environment where techniques like canned openers and cocky and funny are likely to shine. Once you get passed the opener, you'll need to build enough of a connection that you can eventually go somewhere more private with her. One canned approach to this is asking the following 3 questions to elicit her core values:

1. "If you had to choose one thing you need to have in life in order to feel life is worthwhile, what would that be. "(This can also be broken down to, "what do you enjoy doing?")
2. "What would that allow you to do" (or, "describe your perfect scenario doing that.") Listen to her answer, and repeat it all back to her

3. "If you could experience that perfect scenario of doing that, how would that feel inside?" (or if it's something she's actually done, "when you did that, how did you feel inside?")

After she describes how it would feel, you can say, "while you were saying that, I'll bet you felt it inside. See, in just one minute we've fulfilled your life goal. I guess you'll have to come up with a new one." This should be said in a fun way. And please remember, I'm just giving an example of canned material, not advocating its use. Much of this book is devoted to coming up with deep connected conversations in the moment. You don't need to use canned material to be successful. But as I mentioned above, in a noisy club or bar, this is one way to get through the approach so you can move to the next step.

Once you've made a connection with the woman you're interested in, then you want to get her someplace quieter. You can say something like, "hey, I'm having a great time talking to you. There's a coffee place across the street. Let's go over there for a minute and I can tell you about the time I wrestled a lion." If she's with a group of friends, you can say, "hey guys, I think your friend really likes me. I'm gonna let her go buy me a coffee across the street. We'll be right back." Notice that you're not going too far, so it's non-threatening. It's important that you don't lose comfort or you'll be back to square one. It's also important that her friends aren't interfering, so they have to feel like what's going on is ok and their friend will be safe.

Once you're alone with her, you can get into the type of deeper, more connected conversation we discuss later in this book. It's time to build attraction, and relating to her feelings is a great way to do that. We'll go into all of that in greater detail later on.

Meeting women online

This is a vast topic, but I'm not going to spend much time on it. I think you'll improve your skills much faster if you push yourself to meet women in the real world. That said, a lot of women use online dating services to meet men. There's no harm in putting your profile on a few of these and seeing what happens. If you choose to do this, I have a few quick tips.

When you create your online profile, don't try to impress her. This is what every other guy is doing. You want to stand out. Be a character. Create a profile that is an amped up version of yourself, without sounding like you're bragging. If anything, the online profile is one place where coming off like a selfish jerk or like you're trying to drive her away can be a good approach. Keep in mind, I'm not suggesting that you actually be a selfish jerk, that's just the game you're playing with your profile. Her reaction will be, is this guy for real? This negative approach will often get more responses than the more obvious bragging approach. If you don't believe me, create two profiles, one that's more straightforward and one that's more of a caricature. See what really works.

If you don't think you're good looking enough to attract her with your photo, have a talented friend do a drawing of you and put that up for your picture. Or just do a stick figure. This will stand out among all the photos. It will catch her eye.

Online a fun teasing tone often works well. Joking about some detail of her profile in a fun way will demonstrate that you're not obsessed with making her like you. It shows an abundance mindset rather than a scarcity mindset.

And now the number one most important tip about meeting women online. Get things "offline" as soon as possible. You do not want to be emailing back and forth with her for the next year. You want to meet her in real life. To start, tell her to write you back at your real email address. You can say something like, "here's my email. Write to me and tell me three things about yourself that would make me want to get to know you better." Again, this shows that you aren't desperate. You're the one seeing if she meets your qualifications, not the other way around.

Next, get her phone number. You can say, "I'm too busy to keep up with all my email, give me your phone number." I discuss talking on the phone later in the book, but keep in mind that in this context you won't have much history with her when you make the first phone call. It's a good idea to have things to talk about before you call her. Think about some funny or crazy thing that happened to you recently. Call her up and tell her about it. Then make plans to meet somewhere. You can throw a time constraint in there. For example, "hey, I'm having fun talking but I have to go. We should continue this conversation at (local bar or diner). But I can only meet for 30 minutes . . . in case you turn out to be a psycho." This obviously should be said in a playful way. You can leave off the last part if it doesn't feel natural to the dynamic.

It's a great idea to already have planned something to do after you meet with her. Some party you want to go to, or a gallery opening, or whatever. Then after you've met her at the bar or diner and talked a while, you can say, "I was planning on doing (whatever) right now, you're kind of cool, why don't you tag along?"

Keep in mind, I'm not recommending this approach. I would much prefer that you meet women in real life and follow the steps I lay out in this book for doing so. In fact, we're about to get to approaching women in the real world in the next chapter. But for those who also want to explore the online world, these guidelines will substantially improve your chances of going from the virtual world to the real world, where you can make a real and meaningful connection.

Putting it all together

So we're about to delve into what you say when you approach a woman, but first it was important to think about where and when it makes sense to approach. As you go through the rest of your day, look around you and notice which women seem approachable and which ones don't. Why? Is it possible that some of the ones you deemed unapproachable actually could be approached at another time or place? If someone looks busy, is she really, or is she just killing time? Maybe she'd love to have a conversation instead of sitting around reading her magazine. You'll never know unless you approach. And that's what we're about to do.

> **Assignment # 7**
> **Be aware of time, place, and whether the vibe is right for an approach.**

Approaching

You see the perfect woman. She's standing there waiting for a bus. There's no bus in sight. You think about approaching. But what will you say? What if she rejects you? She must be approached all the time. She doesn't want some stranger bothering her. Then again, she does look friendly.

Oops. Here comes the bus, and there goes your chance. Are you going to meet any women this way? No. Then what does it accomplish. Does it protect you from the sting of failure? Not really. It is failure. You failed to approach, and that hurts as much or more than if you had approached and gotten a chilly reception. You've learned nothing and gained nothing. We need to build and grow, not stall and stumble.

Life is short. It's happening right now. Each moment that passes is a moment that's lost forever. You can spend your time trying and learning, or you can spend your time not trying and always failing. Let's give it a try and see what we learn. You see her. You walk up. You open your mouth and say . . . what?

The death of pickup lines

I have good news and bad news. The pickup line is dead. Actually, it never worked that well, but these days pickup lines are considered tacky, and that's just not the impression you want to make. Also, most women have heard more than their fair share of pickup lines. You don't want to be lumped with all the other poor slobs that tried to pick her up with a dumb line. She deserves more than that, and you're smarter than that.

The rise of the canned "opener"

With the death of the pickup line has come its handy replacement, the opener. Instead of a dumb line, the opener is usually an open-ended question or statement meant to initiate conversation. These are helpful, but there are two big problems. First, thanks to the internet, everyone is using the same openers over and over. If you use one, and she's heard it before, you will be pegged as a pickup artist. This is not the impression you want to make. The second problem with openers is that you have to remember them. The fewer things you have to memorize the better, since you're going to be nervous as it is. I don't want you worrying about forgetting your canned opener. And I definitely don't want you pulling out a list of canned openers and reading from it in front of her.

One popular form of opener is the opinion opener. It works like this. You see a group of women, and one in particular catches your eye. You walk up to the group and say something along the lines of, "hey, I have to get back to my friends in a second, but I wanted to ask you a question first. Should the end of the toilet paper roll be in front or in back of the roll?" Let's break this down. The first part, "I have to get back to my friends in a second," is what's known as a time constraint. It prevents the group from thinking, "oh no, who is this guy and how long is he going to stay?" The next part gets their interest, "I wanted to ask you a question." This can also be phrased, "I need your opinion, it's a matter of life and death," or "I need a female opinion on something." Next comes the thing you ask for their opinion on. It can be anything really. Funny is good, here, like the example I gave about the toilet paper. Other popular opinion openers are "which do you do first, brush or floss" (attributed to Neil "Style" Strauss, author of "The Game") and "who lies more, women or men?" (attributed to Mystery, another master pickup artist). Again, I have to warn you that thanks to the internet, as well as Mystery's television show The Pickup Artist, these opinion openers are getting used a lot.

If you come up with your own opener, it is worth testing out and trying. But don't rely on them all the time. Any question that gets her attention and sparks her interest, and leaves room for her to answer with more than a yes or no, is a good start. Really, anything can be an opener. It's much more important what your body language, tonality, and overall vibe is when you approach than what you actually say. If you have an original opener that works for you, great. But it's always good to have a plan B. That plan B is a little more spontaneous than canned material, and I believe this added spontaneity can give the approach some genuine positive energy and excitement.

The spontaneous opener

Instead of using a canned opener, you can be flexible enough to come up with a spontaneous opening question or statement in the moment. Something that sounds fresh because it is. It's like an instantaneous gift from you to her. For example, you see a woman in the bookstore over by the romance novels. You could go up and say, "I've never read a romance novel, if I were to start, which one is your favorite?" Now that might seem like an overly personal question, but if she actually answers you'll be able to follow up by asking why that's her favorite, what does she like about it, and so on. Or you could tell her the kinds of books you usually read and why you like that genre. Soon the conversation is flowing on its own. Now we're going to improve on this in a bit, but for now I just want you to think about things you can say that will elicit more than yes or no. They are open ended, and they flow naturally from the setting you're in.

Let's take another example. You see a woman walking down the sidewalk, past a movie theater. She's looking at the movie posters. You stop and say, "I read a review of that one, it was pretty favorable." This is fairly open ended. You're not asking a question, but you are opening a conversation. If she wants to follow up, it's easy. She can ask about what the review said. If she just grunts and walks off, no big deal. Remember your abundance mindset. Live and learn, and move on.

Ok, one more example, then we start improving these openers. This one doesn't use a question, but rather a story. It's a way for you to show your personality and open a conversation. Let's say you're on the train and sit next to a woman. She's reading. The train stops a little too fast as it pulls into the next station. You could say something like, "This guy must be new. I was on a train once where the driver missed a whole station and had to back the train up. People were pounding on his little driver door yelling at him. It was a real scene." If she's interested, she can ask you more about this, or share a story of her own.

Mind you, I don't expect you to use these exact examples. Don't turn these into more canned openers. Use stories from your own life. Make what you say organic to the situation and your own life experience. If it's genuine, you won't have to worry about where to go next with the conversation because it won't be part of a rehearsed script. You'll be living in the moment, interacting on a genuine level. But we still need one more piece of the puzzle.

Once more, with feeling!

So far I've focused on the types of things you'll ask or say to open the conversation. I've given you some patterns that you can follow, plugging in your own experiences and observations of the situation around you. But for this to really work, you need one more element. Feeling.

It is at this point that I must ask any feminists to leave the room; I'm about to make a generalization about women. All clear? Ok, here it is. Most women are really into feelings and emotions. All right, you can come back, feminists.

So how do you inject feeling into the conversation? Let's zip up some of the examples I've already used and take them to the next level. They are still just examples of a concept, not academy award winning scripts. Look for the ideas and patterns behind the words, and apply them to your own situations as you approach women. And remember, it's not so much what you say, it's how you say it. Fun and friendly beats nervous and creepy every time, no matter what words are coming out of your mouth.

Back to one of our examples. You're in the bookstore, she's looking at romance novels. You walk up. Or better still, you observe which direction she's walking, and place yourself in that path so she walks up to you instead of vice versa. So there she is. You turn to her with a smile and say, "you know, I've always felt I was missing out on something by not reading romance novels, every woman I know seems to love them."

Ok, what have you just done? First, you've opened a conversation. Congratulations. Second, you've done it with something relevant to the current situation, so it doesn't feel like a canned come on. Third, you mentioned this *feeling* you have of missing out on something. Instead of the more sterile approach of announcing that you've never read one, you've added the *feeling* of having missed out on something. You've shown a genuine interest in something that she is interested in. This is good stuff. By attaching a feeling to the situation, you are more likely to get her interest. Don't ask me why that works, it just does. Fourth, you've told her that you know other women. In other words, you are not a pathetic loser. That's also good stuff. Instant validation. In fact, you've told her that you know these other women well enough to know what they like to read. And you actually care about what the women in your life are interested in. That probably distinguishes you from about 99% of the men she knows and meets. And finally, you went for the bonus point by dropping the word "love" in there. Do you see how all of this works together to make her more

58

interested in pursuing the conversation? Do you see how much better this is than a pickup line or canned opener about toilet paper or dental floss?

You don't have to do all these things when you open, or even in the course of the conversation, I'm just pointing them out so when you examine your own openers you can see what you got right, and where there might have been room for improvement. The key element here was that you related to something about her, and you did it with feeling and emotion. That's the gold. Do at least that much in every opening you make, and your ability to start conversations with great women will escalate dramatically. Let me repeat that. Relate your opening to something about her, and do so with genuine feeling. Think about that a second before moving on.

Ok, let's revisit our second example and see if we can spice it up. You see a woman looking at movie posters. You stop and say, "I would *love* to see that one, I read a great review of it last week and I've been *thinking about it* ever since." Wow. How can she resist, she has to ask you what the review said. You don't have to ask her a question to get the conversation started, she's going to ask you the question. You put real emotion into this, and you related it to her and the current situation. Solid gold.

Bear in mind, your goal at this point is not to get her to go see the movie with you, your goal is to have a conversation. But if things progress, you've already planted the seed for your first date. Smart! I shouldn't even have given you that advanced tip this early. But there it is. Plant date ideas into your first conversation and make your life easier later when you actually want to get together with her again.

Ok, let's get back to the main concept we're exploring here, relating to the situation, and doing so with feeling. How about the third example. You're on the jerky train next to the woman reading. You say, "This guy is starting to *worry* me. I hope he's not the same guy who was driving the train last week."

"Why what happened last week," she asks. Or she just ignores you and stares at her book. I'm guessing she can't resist asking. But you'll never know unless you try. So try! If she does ignore the statement, go to another unrelated statement or question aimed at starting a conversation. If it works, she will come back to the original opening statement and ask about the driver from last week. If it doesn't work, learn from it. Build and grow. Keep trying. Every once in a while you run into the girl whose cat just died. But more often than not, you'll run into the girl who is friendly and open to you.

What are you going to say next?

Ok, so you opened with whatever. Maybe it was brilliant, maybe it was lame, but amazingly she's talking to you. You related it to her and the situation you're both in right now. You conveyed emotion, or a feeling. You conveyed confidence and enthusiasm. But what if the conversation falters? Now what? You already used your opening line. Hellllllp!

Calm down. The number one reason conversations stall out is that you are not listening well enough. Listening and then picking up on what she is saying will result in a conversation that is more meaningful. It will also keep you genuinely interested in the conversation, not just going through the motions.

The number two reason conversations stall out is that you didn't direct the conversation toward the wide-open field but instead got stuck down a blind alley. You want a conversation that is expandable, that can go in many directions. Let's explore these concepts further.

Listening to her

One of the most common mistakes people make in any conversation is to think about what they want to say next instead of actually listening to what the other person is saying. The other person is like an egg timer; when it bings then it's your turn to talk. Now you are the egg timer and they are thinking about what they want to say while you blab on. Then *bing*, it's their turn again. This is not a conversation, this is dueling monologs. Frequently these conversations are the same one's she's had a million times. Where do you go to school, what are you studying, where do you work, blah blah blah. Never have a conversation like this during an approach again. Ever. It is pointless and boring. You are done with pointless and boring. It's time to live. Once you've built a connection and attraction it's ok to fall back on these, because you're genuinely interested in learning more about her. But as an approach they stink. You'll have much more success if you engage in the type of conversation she isn't used to having with someone she just met. Be the exception to the rule. Be the guy who stands out. Be the one who isn't just making small talk but is genuinely interested and listening to what she says.

Listening is a skill, and it takes practice. Most people don't bother because they think they already know how to listen. What they actually know how to do is listen when they're interested, and pay attention to their own thoughts when they aren't. We need to break that pattern. How?

- ### Look and listen

First, look at her. Looking at someone helps focus our attention on her, and this helps us to listen and pay attention to what she is saying. Look at her eyes. Look at her face. Don't stare, look. It's ok to look away once in a while, but not for too long as this indicates that your thoughts are elsewhere. Eye contact is the first key to good listening. It also amps up attraction, and that's a very good thing to do.

- ### Act like your listening

Second, *act* like you're listening. If you act like you're listening, it's more likely that you will actually listen. Face her. Give nonverbal cues that you are paying attention. React to what she is saying. Nod your head, or smile, or laugh, or gasp. Whatever is appropriate to what she is saying. I'm not telling you to fake like you're listening, I'm telling you to adopt the body language and actions of a person who is in fact listening. And actually listen. Both. At the same time.

- ### Bring your mind back to her

Finally, if you catch your mind working on the problem of what to say next instead of paying attention to what she's saying now, shift your attention back to her. Does that remind you of something? Perhaps it reminds you of meditating, when your mind gets stuck in thoughts, and you let the thoughts float off as your mind comes back to counting the breath. Do you start to see why meditating is a helpful skill? That is not the only reason to meditate, but it sure is a good one. You are training your mind to stay in the moment, not get stuck in thoughts of past or future. You are learning to notice when your mind drifts, and to gently bring it back to the moment. Stay here, now. Be in this moment. Listen to what she is saying with your eyes, your body language, and your mind. Stay present.

During those times when your mind absolutely insists on doing some thinking, let it think of questions to ask based on what she is saying, instead of just thinking about what you want to say next. Focus on the feeling or emotion behind what she is saying. This will train your mind to focus on what she is saying now, and allow you to say something that demonstrates that focus. It will also get you thinking in terms of feelings and emotions.

If while she's talking you think of a question, that's fine. Go back to paying full attention to her, don't just keep repeating the question in your brain. You might think up a new question, or you might realize the point of what she's saying is something other than what you initially picked up on. Stay with her, not with your internal chatter.

See how this is better than just living in your own thoughts and responding to her with something irrelevant to what she just said? When it's your turn to talk you'll say something that really shows you paid attention, not just to what she said, but to what she was feeling. I can't tell you how important that is. It will distinguish you from the tons of chumps that just came up to her trying to serve their own agenda, never caring enough to find out who she really is. You will not believe how big a difference this makes till you try it out for yourself. So try it out yourself.

And one more tip. Don't interrupt her. Let her finish her thought, then you talk. There's no rush. Let the conversation flow at its own pace, don't try to rush it or control it. You need to let go and be part of the conversation. If you run out of time, then you'll make plans to continue the conversation later, at which time you'll already have things you've been wanting to talk about.

Wow, that was a lot of instructions. You might want to go back over that. When you're done, lets take a look at how a conversation could go, based on the first example of the girl in the bookstore.

Back to the bookstore

You: You know, I've always felt I was missing out on something by not reading romance novels, every woman I know seems to love them.

Her: Well, mostly they're just fluff, but there are a few good ones.

You: So which do you prefer, the fluffy ones or the "good" ones? (This is said jokingly, with a smile)

Her: Well, the fluffy ones are fun, but the "good" ones are better written.

You: Maybe you could recommend one fluffy one and one good one, but don't tell me which is which.

I'll read them both and see if I can tell the difference.

See how this flows? See how it's fun? You are being natural and light and playful. Joking around as though you are with a friend. This will put her at ease. It isn't needy. It isn't seedy. It's friendly. This is by far the best way to get things started. Allow the conversation to flow along naturally, pay attention to what she's saying, ask open ended questions, or make statements that allow her to ask an open ended question, and act the way you would with a friend. Do all that, and I guarantee you your success rate will shoot up through the roof. Women are not used to this from strangers, and it will get their attention. It will also make you feel more relaxed and more confident. Being relaxed and confident are incredibly important and incredibly attractive, but just sitting there trying to be relaxed and confident won't accomplish much. Following the steps we are going through will make you genuinely feel and radiate relaxed confidence.

Keeping it light

I want to point out a few things. Some guys think that by listening for feelings and emotions, or relating feelings or emotions, the conversation somehow has to get heavy. If that's the direction it flows, that's fine, but the conversation can stay fun and light too. The point of listening for feelings and emotions is to find something to relate to. It can be something simple like in the example above. She likes fluffy books, whatever that means, and better written ones. This isn't heavy stuff and isn't all that revealing, but you know more about her than you did a few seconds ago. It's something to build on. In the response, you show that you can appreciate both, and turned it into a game.

Keep it fun, that's what this is all about, especially early in the conversation. But stay tuned in to what she is saying. Allow yourself to be open to the feelings and emotions behind the words, and work your own feelings and emotions into the conversation to make things more alive and meaningful. Make a connection and build on it. This doesn't have to be heavy. You aren't going to psychoanalyze her. You are just looking to find a connection. That connection is going to happen at the emotional level.

Putting it into practice

So you've been talking for a few minutes. Your heart may be pounding but you're ignoring that and just paying attention to the conversation, letting it flow. Better still, maybe your heart isn't pounding, you feel relaxed and confident. Now what? It's time to take things to the next level.

But before we get there, I have another assignment for you. Don't worry, you're not going to do the full approach yet, unless you want to. We're taking baby steps. What I want you to do for now is go up to a woman and ask any simple question. For example, "do you know what time it is," or "excuse me, are there any good places to eat around here?"

> **Assignment # 8**
> Approach women and ask for the time, or a place to eat, or some other simple question. Listen to the answer.

Something that can be answered simply. If you ask for the time, it might be a good idea to stick your Rolex in your pocket.

Listen to the answer you get. That might seem easy, but if she tells you the time and walks off, and you can't remember what time she said, you weren't listening. This exercise will get you more comfortable with approaching women, and will get you listening. Get that part down and the rest will be so much easier.

If this seems too easy, go try it. You might feel some initial approach anxiety. It is a hurdle you need to work past. You need to feel for yourself what happens when you get past that, open your mouth and talk. You need to work on the tone of your voice and your body language. This is an easy way to work on these crucial elements.

If it really is too easy for you, feel free to practice the conversational techniques we've been discussing and try to get some emotion in there. That's where we're heading anyway, so if you want to start now that's fine. If the conversation fizzles, don't worry. Just say, "nice talking to you, maybe I'll see you around" and move on. We'll get to techniques for keeping the conversation flowing soon. In the next step on our journey we'll learn to open up the conversation rather than steering it down a blind alley.

> **Extra Credit!**
> Approach women and start a conversation. Make it relate to the situation, and bring in emotion. See what happens

Pump it up!

Ok I lied. We're not ready for the next step yet. First of all, if you didn't do that last assignment yet, do it. I want that under your belt before we move on. Approach anxiety is part of the process. You need to get used to it, and used to working past it, making the approach, and talking in a calm, confident way. It's also good to get used to talking to women without any expectation of making them fall in love with you on the spot. Stop attaching to the result and you're more likely to achieve it. If that doesn't make sense just yet, don't worry; this stuff works whether you understand it or not.

So before we get to the next step—keeping the conversation flowing—I need to ask you some questions. What do you really enjoy in your life? What makes you happiest? What are your hobbies? What types of books do you read, what movies do you see, what music do you like? What are some of your happiest memories? When have you felt really great?

That's a lot of questions. Did you think about them all or just read through the list. Go back and answer each and every question before we move on, because we've got more work to do. We're taking this a step at a time and we do not skip steps. Right?

Right!

If you've thought through the questions, next I want you to make a list of positive feelings and emotions. For example, you can feel strong, confident, happy, warm, loved, etc. Make this list of positive feelings, then go through the list and relate each of those feelings or emotions to a specific time and place when you felt that way. These could be just "titles" to the stories in your life that relate to these feelings. Each of these stories will be fodder for conversation. Look for the broader themes in those stories. What were those positive experiences about? Adventure? Testing yourself? Experiencing something new? Going deeper into something than you'd gone before? A realization? A change in the way you viewed something? Just having a blast? Experiencing true freedom? Fill a page with story "titles" and the positive feelings you associate them with.

What we are doing is building a list of stories that have real meaning to you. These are not the old stale stories people usually tell when making small talk or meeting someone for the first time. This is not "where do you work . . . what are you studying" style conversation. This is stuff that is important and alive. It means something to you. When you talk about these events in your life, your eyes light up, you become animated, you reveal something true about yourself. You talk about *feelings and emotions*, the stuff that women love to talk about. This is your magic list, the raw material you can dip into to take your conversations to the next level, and keep them going.

So how do we transition to these stories? Well, that's where the feelings, emotions, and themes come in. But first, we have to listen to what she's saying. What feeling, emotion, or theme is she communicating? What is she telling you about herself?

Back to the bookstore

When we left off, the girl in the bookstore was saying how she likes the fluff as well as the well-written stuff. What does that tell you about her? She has a fun side and a serious side. She's not afraid to let her hair down and have fun. She's got taste, but she's not a snob. You could pick up on any of these and then go a few directions with it. You could make a statement that shows you paid attention and heard the feeling or emotion behind the statement. You could relate it to a story in your life that shows a similar feeling or emotion. Or, you could make a statement that shows you admire the trait being revealed by what she said. All of these are good options. You need to sense where you are in the conversation to know what direction to go. This is not something where you're going to stop and think about it. It's just going to happen. Look for the feeling, emotion, theme, or trait in her statement, and flow from there naturally. Let's go back to the conversation and see how this can work, demonstrating each option in turn:

You: So which do you prefer, the fluffy ones or the
       "good" ones?

Her: Well, the fluffy ones are fun, but the "good" ones are better written.

You: Option 1: So you've got taste but you're not a snob.

Option 2: Sounds like you keep your options open. I'm like that too. I play classical guitar and electric guitar. I love the complexity of the classical music, and I love the energy of jamming out some rock n' roll.

Option 3: I admire that about you. So many people try to impress everyone with their taste, but you're not afraid to read something just for fun.

Now where do you go from here? Using the first response, the key concept is fun over formality. She's not afraid to just have fun. You can say anything that plays on that theme. Or move to another subject altogether.

If you want to use option 3, think of a time that you did something just for fun, good taste be damned. To stay with the flow of the conversation, it could involve something considered lowbrow. For example, you could say, "That reminds me of the time I was thrifting with a friend and we found a bin of old pulp novels. The covers were hilarious, and we flipped through the books and read each other some choice quotes. People were peeking down the aisle at us wondering what was so funny. I ended up buying a few of the most outrageous ones, I'll have to show them to you some time."

Ok, let's back up. What just happened. Our hero, you, was prepared. By thinking through different positive experiences in your life, and thinking about what feelings you associate with those times, you've got a ready store of key experiences to share in your conversation. First, you listened to what she was saying. Next, you explicitly noticed the trait that she demonstrated with what she said. This shows that you're listening. In the process you also mentioned that you actually have a friend. You do not live in a cave. That's good. Finally, if things go well and you're on a date, you've planted an important seed. When you want a reason for her to come to your place, you can say, "Hey, why don't we go to my place and I'll show you those pulp novels I told you about. They're amazing." See how one thing naturally flows to the next? See how this all makes sense? It's not awkward, it's not forced, and therefore it's not going to put her off.

In option 3, not only did you show that you were listening, you told her you admire her. You don't just like her because she's cute, you admire something that is specific to her. There are lots of good-looking women, but she's got something special and you appreciate it. Believe me, that's going to get her attention.

What about option 2? In option 2 you relate the trait, feeling, or emotion to something in your life. This tells her something about you, something that resonates with what she just told you about herself. You can continue talking about that, go back to what she was talking about, or move on to something new.

So which one is the right option? Really, they are all part of the same thing, which is relating to her, showing you like something that is unique about her, and showing her something unique about you. You are listening to the words and the ideas, themes, emotions and feelings behind those words. You are staying in that place with her where you are both slowly opening up. Do you see how different this is from just standing there and asking, "what's your name, where do you work, how do you like that, what made you decide to get into that, blah blah blah." This is the real deal, you are relating with another human, you are connecting. It doesn't have to be heavy or serious, it just has to be real and alive.

By listening to her and responding to what she's saying, you end up in a much more engaging and meaningful conversation than you'd ever have starting with a pickup line or canned opening. You've noticed a specific feeling, emotion, or theme behind her words. Now you can talk about other things that make you feel that way, other times you had a similar emotion, or other events in your life that illustrate the same theme. You can explore the theme in her life, with a question like, "what are other areas where you appreciate both the fluff and the fine stuff?" You can also tell her you admire the trait she has revealed before further exploring the theme or moving on to a new one. There are many directions the conversation can go, so you won't get stuck down a blind alley. You've made an emotional connection, and you've opened the conversational possibilities, all in one fell swoop. Now the conversation is both meaningful and expandable.

This is so important, I'm going to give you another example. Don't get hung up on the words; focus on the flow. We're back on the train:

You: This guy is starting to worry me. I hope he's not the same guy who was driving the train last week.

Her: Why what happened last week?

You: The driver kept starting and stopping the train, then he missed a whole station and had to back the train up. People were pounding on his little driver door yelling at him. It was pretty chaotic.

Her: Wow, that does sound pretty bad.

You: Well, it still beats driving, at least you can get in some reading. Is that a good book?

Her: It's pretty dry. It's about global warming.

You: Ah, one more good reason to take the train. I think that's really cool of you. A lot of people talk about global warming but few really understand it. You're taking the time to dig deeper and educate yourself. And you take the train, which means you're part of the solution, not part of the problem. Very cool.

There are a lot of places you could go from here. You could talk about global warming, but that's a bit of a dead end, and a bit of a bummer. You could talk more about crazy train drivers but that's pretty much dead already. A better bet would be to build on the idea of practicing what you preach, or the idea of educating yourself on a topic of interest, instead of just skimming the surface. Either one is a broad topic that could go many different directions. In other words, it's expandable. What's something you found interesting and took the time to learn more about. How did that feel? Did digging deeper reveal something important? Or, is there something in your own life that you feel strongly about and manage to practice in some way? Hopefully this theme triggers one of the stories from the list of life stories you made earlier. Or reminds you of one not on the list. This conversation could branch in a lot of different directions, all of them meaningful and expandable. It can grow and flow organically, not fizzle out and die.

Please note, listening and relating like this does not mean compromising yourself. You are still you, you still have your own feelings, emotions, etc. But you are coming from that place where you are in touch with your own feelings, and connecting with her by being aware of her feelings and emotions. You don't adopt her feelings and emotions, you are aware of them and relating them to your own. This is so important we need to dig into it even deeper. This is the heart of what we are doing, and it is how you are going to build a connection with her that will blossom endlessly.

Find the emotion, theme, feeling, or trait. Notice, admire, and relate

There's something important you should realize at this point. The words that are being spoken in these examples—and in your actual conversations—are secondary to the feelings and emotions and broader themes behind them. And these in turn are secondary to the fact that you are having a fun, interesting, comfortable conversation, which will show in your body language and nonverbal cues. You are connecting and building attraction. That is the key. The important thing is that she isn't sitting there thinking, "what does this freak want, why is he talking to me?" She's in the conversation. You're both floating in a bubble together, letting it fly where it will. It's fun. It's an adventure. It's alive!

So even if you think the example conversations are a bit goofy, that's ok. That just means those aren't the conversations you would have. But what are the conversations that you would have? Go back to your list of positive life events. Go back to the feelings, emotions, and themes that relate to those memories. These are easy to remember because they come from your real life, unlike canned lines. They will come to mind naturally as you listen to what she is saying and look for the feelings, emotions, and themes. Find some trait of hers, notice it, admire it, and relate it to something in your own life. These don't have to happen all at once. They don't have to happen in response to the same trait. But keep working on all of them in all your approaches.

Find the emotion, feeling, or trait. Notice, admire, and relate. Find the emotion, feeling, or trait. Notice, admire, and relate.

It's not a great poem, but it should be your approach mantra. And please don't treat this as a set of rules or a flowchart. Conversations are far too dynamic for that. These are concepts that you need to embody and practice. Make them part of you, and your conversations will flow. And remember, your connection to her is through shared emotional states. Shared interests are great, but not essential. Shared emotional states are what you're after.

At first this takes practice. It is not the way people usually talk. Most conversations exist on the surface of the words and don't dive below that surface. Notice, admire, and relate, and you are going to connect. Your conversation is going to take on a life of its own. So while it takes practice, the practice will pay off. Bear in mind, it's ok to just make small talk if the small talk is flowing. You don't have to dive deeper right away. Get her comfortable. Get yourself comfortable. Then slowly amp it up, making the conversation more meaningful, and keeping it expandable. Notice, admire, and relate. This will allow you to relax and listen completely. The conversation will go on autopilot for long periods of time. And when it looks like it's losing altitude, you ask more open ended questions or make a statement that leads to questions. You can even change the topic completely. If things are really going well, you could ask her what she values in a relationship, and then later in the conversation work in stories that show you can demonstrate those values. Get into more feelings, emotions, and themes that expand the conversational options and get you back flying high again. Find the emotion, feeling, or trait. Notice, admire, and relate.

Time for another assignment. First, we've covered a lot in this chapter and the one before it. Re-read them both. Next, we revisit the extra credit assignment from last chapter, only now it's not extra credit. It's show time! Try some more approaches, only this time instead

Assignment # 9
Approach women
and open a
conversation. Make
eye contact, and
really listen to what
she says. Keep it
flowing as long as
you can. Let your
body language
show that you're
comfortable and
engaged.

of asking for the time or a place to eat, you're going to make an opening statement or question that fits the situation. Don't worry about how long you keep the conversation going. Just open and get a response. If it fizzles there, that's fine. Just say, "nice talking to you," or "I'll see you around," and move on. If the conversation does take off, great. This is like learning ping-pong. At first, just hitting the ball is tricky. Then you try to get it over the net. Then you try to volley a few times. Then you get good enough to play a game. And then the real fun begins.

So right now we're trying to volley a bit. Make sure you are listening to what she says. Make sure you face her and keep good, natural eye contact. Your body can be side by side with hers rather than facing hers, but you should be looking at her, not looking around like you're bored. Make sure you keep things open; don't go down a blind alley. That's a lot to keep in mind. Keep at it and all this will become natural. Oh, and you get bonus points if you work in something you admire about her. It can be anything *other than* physical beauty. It does not have to come from something she says, it can be her sense of style, a nice ring, a book she's carrying that you've read, a sticker on her backpack. Anything. If it tells you anything about who she is, notice it and admire it. Then keep the conversation flowing. Don't pause after the statement of admiration or things will feel awkward. Admire and keep going. You could relate the trait you just admired to something from your own life, or something you admire in a friend you have. Again, this could be as simple as, "hey, I love that watch. My friend Jenny is always telling me I need to learn to accessorize, but I like to leave that to the experts."

Triple bonus points if you don't drool, trip, fart, spill something on yourself, spill something on her, or freak out and start yelling, "I am the Lizard King, I can do anything!" Just stay cool and talk, just like when you're talking to a friend. Listen to what she's saying and flow from there. It's going to be great.

When you've done more practice approaches and you see for yourself that this really does work, you're ready for the next step, turning up the attraction. This will involve making a statement of intent, getting your nonverbal cues together, and the secret ingredient—the thing that's going to get her more attracted and feeling more positive about you—the magic touch.

Turn it up to eleven!

You're working on your conversational skills, remembering to look for ways to make the conversation meaningful and expandable. You've got a mental list of life events you associate with various feelings, emotions, and themes. It's starting to make sense. You're enjoying talking to women more, they are enjoying talking to you more. It's even spreading to other aspects of your life. You find talking to people in general is more fun, because you can always practice your skills and learn more about them. Life is good. In fact, you could stop right there and already have done a lot to improve your skills at meeting women. But we don't settle for good around here. We don't even settle for great. This is the Zen approach. We are always practicing, always going deeper. This is a journey and we have only just begun. In many ways the rough part is over. But the best is yet to come.

In this chapter we'll learn some key concepts that will help you intensify the attraction and move things to the next level. You'll do this by letting her know what's on your mind, sending the right nonverbal cues, and giving her the "magic touch." I don't know about you, but I'm excited. Let's get started.

Statement of Intent

Up to this point, you've let her know at least one thing you admire about her, either directly or just by the fact that you are listening to her and paying attention to the feelings and emotions behind her words. You've built rapport.

But don't assume that she knows you find her attractive. Don't assume she knows you would like to date her. For all she knows, you just want to be friends. Do not fall into the "let's just be friends" trap. There is nothing worse than maintaining a friendship with a woman while secretly harboring the hope that somehow, someday, it will blossom into a romance. It rarely works out that way. The only way to get on the right road is to steer the car in the right direction from the very start. Go too far down Friendship Lane, and you'll find there's no turning back. You'll avoid that bad trip with a Statement of Intent.

So what is a Statement of Intent? Very simple. Once she starts showing some attraction, you tell her that she's sexy. But don't worry, we aren't going to just blurt it out and leave it at that. You will link her sexiness to a specific trait. I'll explain exactly how soon, but first, let's go back and review some important skills you've developed that we are going to call upon now to make this work and not feel or sound weird.

We've discussed how important it is to really listen to her when she talks. You learned to listen not just to the words, but to listen for the feelings, emotions, and themes that were behind the words. Ideally, you told her at some point that you admire some specific quality she displayed in what she said, even if that quality was not explicitly stated. So if she says she likes to play volleyball with her friends, you

81

could have said, "I really like that about you that you've found a way to combine getting healthy and spending time with your friends." You've found an idea behind the specific activity of playing volleyball with her friends, you've summed it up in a way that shows a specific trait that she has and that you admire. And the conversation could flow many directions from there. You could talk about trying to balance different things in life, or discuss ways to incorporate being healthy into other parts of your life, or whatever. You're living your mantra, "find the emotion, feeling, or trait. Notice, admire, and relate."

But now the conversation has gone on for a few minutes. How many? Unless you carry a stopwatch, it doesn't matter because your perception of time is going to be very distorted anyway. You probably shouldn't wait more than twenty minutes before making the Statement of Intent, but that's a very flexible rule. The sooner you can do it, the better. In fact you can do a Statement of Intent instead of just doing the "I really admire that about you" statement if you feel like you're already clicking. If not, the series of events will most likely be:

1. you approach
2. you open with a statement that leads her to ask a question, or you ask an open ended question
3. you focus on feelings and emotions, the conversation continues, and she reveals some trait
4. you acknowledge the trait and either admire it or relate it to something similar in your own life, or both

5. the conversation continues, perhaps it shifts gears into some new territory. She's showing some signs of attraction or interest in you, and she reveals another trait. That's when you make your Statement of Intent.

Please do not obsess over these steps. This is not a script, a set of rules, or a checklist that must be followed every time. It is how things will often flow, but if a step is skipped or steps merge and things are going well, do not panic. Just go with the flow. The important thing is you are connecting with her and things are going well before you make the Statement of Intent.

So here's a sample conversation. We're back on the train, and you've been talking a bit. You ask her what she's reading:

You: Well, riding the train still beats driving, at least you can get in some reading. Is that a good book?

Her: It's pretty dry. It's about global warming.

You: Ah, one more reason to take the train, make less pollution. I think that's admirable of you. A lot of people talk about global warming but few really understand it. You're taking the time to dig deeper and educate yourself.

Her: Well, I'm not digging that deep, it's just one book. I just feel really strongly about the environment and I didn't want to sound like an idiot when I talk about it. [Note there are a couple of feelings here, feeling strongly about the environment, and feeling the urge to not come off as an idiot. Now here comes the Statement of Intent]

You: I think that's really sexy the way you're interested enough to dig deeper, and ambitious enough to do something about it. So many people just wish they knew more about a subject and leave it at that.

From there you could go lots of places. You could relate it to something in your life that you feel strongly about, or that you studied deeply, or you could ask her what she's learning in the book that she didn't realize before. You can go back to the feeling of not wanting to seem like an idiot, and joke that you avoid that problem by wearing glasses. Whatever you do, keep things flowing. Make your Statement of Intent, and then *immediately* continue on with the conversation as if nothing happened. Be smooth with this and it won't feel or sound awkward. Do NOT stop after the Statement of Intent or it will feel like a car crash. She'll think she's supposed to say "thank you," or to tell you she thinks you're sexy, or something equally awkward. Keep it moving and you'll avoid this problem. Say something, anything. Just keep it flowing.

So here's the secret formula for the Statement of Intent. "I think that's really sexy the way you X," or "I think that's really sexy that you X," where X is some positive trait she has that is unique to her. X is *not* something about how she looks. Do not say, "I think that's really sexy the way your breasts look." That is not a Statement of Intent, that is the end of the conversation, and an invitation to a slap. Do say something along these lines:

- I think that's really sexy that you're so ambitious
- I think that's really sexy the way you speak your mind
- I think that's really sexy that you care enough to try and make a difference
- I think that's really sexy the way you don't give up solving a difficult problem
- I think that's really sexy that you're so adventurous.
- I think that's sexy the way you give in to your wild side.

If you want to try different ways of making the Statement of Intent, be my guest. Instead of "sexy," you could say "attractive," "hot," or something else that conveys your attraction to her. But do me a favor. Try doing the Statement of Intent with the word "sexy" at least once and see what happens. If you don't pause, but rather keep the conversation flowing after the Statement of Intent, you'll find that it gives her the signal that you're interested without making things uncomfortable. You're trying to be subtle and obvious at the same time. She may act like she didn't even hear the "sexy" part, but believe me, she did. A little switch just clicked on in her brain that says, "he's into me, but he's being cool about it." Remember, stay relaxed and natural and keep talking after the Statement of Intent, that is key. Don't put her on the spot. Let her know what direction you're going, and keep on moving.

Assignment time. Don't worry, we're going to practice this one. A lot. All the time in fact. But silently at first. Wherever you are, whatever you're doing, I want you to come up with Statements of Intent that fit the situation. If you're watching a sitcom on TV and a character reveals that she quit her job because her boss was a jerk, think to yourself, "I think that's really sexy that you don't put up with other people's negativity." If you're on the train and a woman walks on with a Greenpeace sticker on her backpack, think to yourself, "I think that's really hot that you care so much about animals" If you see a woman walking down the street talking on a cell phone, think to yourself, "I think that's really attractive the way you make time for your friends, no matter how busy the day gets."

> **Assignment # 10**
> Practice coming up with statements of intent. Remember, there should be some connection, some sign of attraction first, and you need to keep talking after the statement of intent. What would you say next to keep things flowing? Eventually, use a Statement of Intent in a real conversation.

Remember, the purpose of this statement is not to sound like a genius. It is to let her know that **you think she's sexy!** You've met her, started talking, admired something about her, kept the conversation flowing, learned a little more about her, and now you are telling her right out that you think she is sexy. But you're doing it in a way that relates your attraction to some trait other than just physical beauty, and then you continue the conversation in a natural way. She now knows you don't just want to be friends, you want more. But you haven't put her on the spot. She does not need to respond. The conversation can continue, and you can get to know each other better. Yes, this is going to be difficult at first, but I hope you see how valuable it is. You will avoid any ambiguity that could result in her thinking you just want to be friends. If that's ever happened to you before, then you already know it's worth the time spent practicing the Statement of Intent.

Practice coming up with Statements of Intent. Eventually, you're going to find yourself in a conversation and it will feel right to actually use one. I want you to rehearse the Statement of Intent in your head so much that eventually one just pops out in an actual conversation. When that happens, you can take the next step on our journey.

Oh, and if it doesn't happen by itself during the next 10 approaches you make, then I guess you have to force it a few times to get over your fear. Eventually it will feel natural. Whatever it takes to get there, that's what you need to do. Bear in mind, if you've already built a connection before you reach this point, this is an important screening tool. What I mean by that is, you can't just stop the conversation and say, "look, I really like you, but I'm also physically attracted to you. Do you see me as boyfriend material or just friend material." That would obviously be putting her on the spot, and bring things crashing to a halt.

The Statement of Intent is a much more subtle way of conveying the same idea very quickly and in the context of the conversation you're already having. It makes sure you're both on the same level. If immediately after the Statement of Intent she starts running away screaming, either you did it wrong or she just wasn't interested in anything more than friendship. In the first case, keep practicing till it feels natural. In the second case, you're better off finding out now than after a year of frustration that she only sees you as a friend. As painful as it may be to spit out the Statement of Intent, there's no way it's as bad as being stuck in the friend zone when you want so much more.

Now let's polish things up even more. Let's get your nonverbal communication to the same level as your verbal communication, so it's all happening smoothly and naturally.

Nonverbal cues – body language

A great deal of communication happens nonverbally. In fact, Albert Mehrabian— Professor Emeritus of Psychology at UCLA—found that in communications that involve feelings or attitudes, only 7% of the communication comes from spoken words, 38% is from voice tone, and an astounding 55% is from body language. The way you hold yourself and the way you sound are very very important. If you are really in the moment and the conversation is flowing naturally, your nonverbal cues will hopefully be consistent with what you're saying. But if you feel nervous you are likely to show this inadvertently or convey it in the sound of your voice. And this in turn might make her feel nervous. There goes the whole vibe you were trying to build with your conversation.

It's really hard to remember this and remember to listen and remember everything else all at the same time. So practice working on your body language and tone of voice when you're just having normal conversations with friends, co-workers, or whoever. Train yourself to avoid the bad habits, and then you won't have to think about it when the heat is on. Here is a quick list of do's and don'ts.

Do NOT:

- Put your hands in your pockets
- Lean in too close
- Hunch over, or bow
- Face away from her
- Cross your arms
- Move around too much
- Look around at other people instead of her
- Frown

DO:

- Keep your hands out so you can express yourself with them and use them for the "magic touch," which is coming up
- Stand about an arm's length away, or a little farther if she seems uncomfortable. (You can stand closer if you're side by side rather than facing each other)
- Stand with an upright back, shoulders back, good confident posture
- Face your body towards her, or at a slight angle (although during the initial approach, side by side works well)
- Keep your arms open and moving naturally
- Stay still for the most part

- Look right at her, make good natural eye contact
- Smile, laugh, and look interested in what she's saying

Again, this is a lot to keep in mind, so practice it all the time until it's natural. Look at yourself in a full-length mirror or videotape yourself and start talking. See if you break any of these rules. If you do, you know to work on that one. Also, use the video camera or a tape recorder and listen to the sound of your voice. It should be smooth and confident, not hurried and nervous. Pause once in a while when you're talking, don't rush from sentence to sentence. Be confident enough to let your words hang there. Don't talk too fast. Relax and convey confidence with your voice as well as your body.

If rules aren't your thing, this can all be boiled down to the following. Your body language and tone of voice have to communicate two things: confidence and interest. You are a confident person, and you are interested in what the other person is saying. You are giving your undivided attention, and you feel comfortable in the moment. Work on this and all your interactions will be more successful.

Assignment # 11
Work on your body language and voice tone. Communicate confidence and interest with your entire body.

Now we're ready to move on to the big one. This is what will let her know nonverbally that you are interested, and will keep the message of the Statement of Intent alive in her heart and mind.

The Magic Touch – "Kino"

Touch is very magic indeed. It is a very strong nonverbal cue. It does a lot of things at once. It shows interest, it shows connection, and it shows confidence, if you do it right. It also ups the ante. You will want to be very careful with this one. You need to touch in the right place at the right time. In the pickup artist community, touch is referred to as kino. Here's an outline of an interaction, with kino sprinkled in here and there.

Kino Outline:

- You approach, initiate conversation.
- **Kino**: If it feels right, you shake her hand
- She tells you something interesting and positive about herself
- **Kino**: you touch somewhere between elbow and shoulder on her arm
- At the same time as the kino, you say you admire some trait she has demonstrated
- You tell a story about something related to the feeling, emotion, or theme you admired in her
- She says something related to what you said and reveals more about herself

- **Kino**: you touch the same spot as before, or if it feels right, perhaps take her hand and squeeze it
- Your turn to talk, building on what she said.
- Her turn to talk, she reveals more
- **Kino**: arm or hand. At the same time you make your Statement of Intent, then immediately keep the conversation flowing with more talk.

And so on. To summarize, the kino is like a little show of appreciation for something she has done or said. It's the gift of touch. If she reveals a positive trait, or makes a joke, or compliments you, or does anything else you like, you show your appreciation with the magic touch. This, combined with the Statement of Intent, helps make your intentions clear, but in a non-threatening way. As long as you are confident in the way you touch her, she will not think it's creepy. She'll just assume you're one of those touchy feely kind of guys. If you are natural and calm about it, she will be ok with it. In fact more than ok. People like to be touched, as long as the circumstances are right.

Don't believe me? Put your left hand on your right arm, between elbow and shoulder. Don't squeeze, just put it there. Feels warm, right? Feels nice. Now imagine if a cute woman that you were really connecting with put her hand there while talking to you. Would you shriek and run away? Or would it make your heart go thump thump? Touch is magic. Touch is powerful. Touch is what will keep the connection and the attraction amplified.

Using a Statement of Intent, good nonverbal cues, and kino will crank up the electricity and intensity of your interaction. Stay in the moment, confident, and real. Make her feel the connection between you, and then let it grow. When you've got all this going on and things are still smooth sailing, you have made substantial progress. You are now ready to close.

But first, yes you guessed it, one more assignment. This one is actually several assignments combined. I assume you've done all the other assignments up to this point.

You've practiced your approach. And you've practiced coming up with Statements of Intent in lots of situations, but so far it's mostly been in your head, with perhaps a few actual real life tries. It's time to put it together and use it in real life along with kino, the magic touch. Remember, there is no such thing as failure as long as you are willing to experiment and learn. Every step you

Assignment # 12
Do some approaches, using kino and statement of intent. Be confident and interested. Make the connection, and watch it grow. This takes practice, so keep at it.

take is a step forward. So go initiate a conversation and within the first 20 minutes make a Statement of Intent. Make sure you keep the conversation flowing, don't pause. Then, during the next approach you do, practice kino. Finally, do an approach where you start some kino early on, do a Statement of Intent, and continue with the kino. Notice, I'm not explicitly telling you to do anything about nonverbal cues. Hopefully, you are staying outwardly confident, and interested in what she is saying. If not, the kino is not going to be well received. Keep playing around with all of these. Try them earlier in the conversation. Try them later. See what works. You need to get a feel for this so it's natural, and the only way to do that is to practice. That's why the only failure is not trying. If you make an approach, it's an opportunity for you to practice and improve.

Don't worry, even if you're awkward with your kino or statement of intent initially, most women will just let it slide. As long as you keep the conversation flowing, things should not get too awkward. Keep practicing this over and over and over. You have to actually get a feel for how this all works, just reading about it is not enough. If things go horribly wrong, you can always bail out by saying, "hey, I need to get back to my friends now but it was nice meeting you." Then think about what worked and what didn't, and where you need to improve. Do another approach and work on your sticking point until you've got it together.

This assignment might feel less like a baby step and more like learning to swim. You have to do a lot of things at the same time. It's going to be a little awkward at first. That's ok. As long as you've built a connection in the beginning, she's going to cut you some slack. Just go for it, and see what you learn. The next time will be easier, and the next time easier still. When it really starts to be natural, then you can start focusing on closing the deal. But before we get there, we need to bring Zen back into the process, and we need to plan for what to do when things don't go perfectly.

Learning and growing

You're working on your approach. You've talked to some interesting women and you're starting to realize that this isn't as hard as you'd imagined it. Most women you approach are pretty friendly. But then you hit one that is decidedly chilly. All you get are one-word answers. Despite your best efforts the conversation keeps stalling out. You try some kino and she shrinks away. You make a statement of intent and her face registers shock and horror. Inside your head a voice starts yelling, "Mayday, Mayday!" Is this the end? Time to give up? Well, before you hit the eject button, I want you to consider the following.

Success versus failure

This is a process. At first, you need to focus on the process, not the results. Keep working on the process and the results will take care of themselves, as long as you pay attention to what you're doing right and wrong, and keep working on improving in all areas. Some things will come easy, others will be harder. Some women you approach will be easier to talk to, some will turn out to be the Ice Princess. You just have to keep at it.

Imagine two students in a Spanish class, Happy and Sadsack. Happy practices Spanish every day, shows up for class on time, pays attention, works on the areas that are most difficult, and makes a little progress every day. He focuses on improving. Meanwhile Sadsack sits in class lost in his own thoughts. He considers every day a failure, because every day is one more day that he is not yet fluent in Spanish. He's too depressed to work on the hard stuff, and after a while he even gives up practicing the parts that come easy. It's all one big failure. A dark cloud follows him wherever he goes.

Now, who is going to get the A and who is going to get the F? If you go into anything with an attitude like Happy's you can't help but succeed, because every day is a success. If you're like Sadsack, then every day is a failure, and this self-fulfilling prophecy just drags you further and further down.

Does attitude matter? You bet. There is no such thing as failure as long as you keep an open mind and keep trying; you will learn from every encounter. Analyze what went right and what went wrong. And keep in mind, every once in a while you're just going to approach someone who absolutely does not want to talk to anyone at that moment. We all have our bad days. It's not your fault. There is a little bit of luck involved in this, but you can't control luck. Work on the things you can work on, leave the rest to fate, and keep a positive attitude, because it really does make a difference.

But what about rejection? That stuff hurts. Yes, rejection hurts, but you cannot be rejected during an approach. You might encounter women that are not interested in where the conversation is heading, or who are truly too busy at the moment to give you the time of day, but that is not a rejection of you. They haven't even had the time to get to know you yet, so how can they reject you? At most they are rejecting your approach, which is helpful to you because now you know you need to work on it more. There is no real rejection here, just lessons.

Some approaches will go easy, some will be hard. Learn from every single one, and don't take it personally.

Study what you did right and wrong

If you're the super organized type, you can keep notes on each encounter. You could even make a transcript of the conversation and figure out where things went off the track and what you could have said to avoid that. You could write down a new conversation where you say the right thing at the point where things fizzled, and keep the conversation going. Or perhaps keep track of when you initiate kino and how successful it is at that point.

If you're a more visual type, you can just sit and daydream all the brilliant things you could have said, and how things could have progressed from there. Don't underestimate the power of this type of thought exercise. By imagining it, you are living it. You are training your mind and you will be better prepared the next time you do an approach. But please, only imagine positive outcomes. No negative thinking here, it will get you nowhere. Picture success, and you will have success.

Don't take it personally – don't attach

If the conversation bombs it's very easy to beat yourself up afterwards. "I'm such a loser, why did I say that?" Stop that type of thinking dead in its tracks and replace it with a logical positive response, like, "I can't believe I broke through my fear of approaching, that's great." Pat yourself on the back for all the things you did right. Did you make eye contact? Did you get a chance to practice your kino? Did she give you any positive vibe at all? Did you learn anything from the encounter? If so, that's great. That is success. Don't attach to each and every approach that doesn't go perfectly. Don't attach to each and every woman you talk to. Let go and move on.

Two Monks & a Beautiful Woman

There's a story of two monks, one young, one old, that were walking through the woods when they came to a river. There was a beautiful woman standing at the bank of the river. She told the monks she was afraid to cross, as she might slip and the current could carry her downstream. The two monks were celibate and had taken vows never to touch a woman. But the old monk sensed the woman's anxiety and felt compassion for her. He lifted her onto his back and carried her to the other side of the river, setting her gently down.

The beautiful woman thanked him and went on her way, and the monks continued on their journey. But the young monk was shocked at having seen the old monk break his vow so nonchalantly. After three hours of walking and mulling it over, he could not contain himself any longer. He burst out,

"Tell me old man, how could you break your sacred vow? How could you allow sensuality to tempt you from your spiritual path? How could you carry her on your back, with her thighs wrapped around your waist, her breasts against your back, and her arms around your neck? Tell me, old man, why did you carry that young woman?"

The older monk replied, "I put her down three hours ago, why are *you* still carrying her?"

Don't be like the young monk, stewing and fretting and attaching to this woman and that. Each woman you talk to is a gift. Sometimes you get a gift you didn't expect, or one you didn't like, but it's still a gift. No big deal. Don't obsess over every approach. Live and learn and move on. Don't keep carrying the beautiful young woman three hours later. Set her down and walk on. If you live in the past, you'll miss the present. Live every moment.

You will get better and better

With the right attitude, you will be learning and improving, probably faster than you expected. One early revelation is how friendly most women are when you approach them in an open and honest way. Get the vibe right and the words almost don't matter. In those first few moments, they are curious to see why you are approaching, what you are going to say. Are you just a creep? Some guy trying to pick them up? Are you the prince they've always dreamed of, come to rescue her from her dull day? Who are you and what do you want? There's a lot of possibility in those first few moments, and it really can be exhilarating. Ride that wave of excitement, stay in the flow of the moment. See where it takes you.

It just keeps getting better and better, easier and easier. Think of yourself 3 months from now, after hundreds of approaches. Think how grateful you'll be to the you who sits here right now, preparing to embrace that 3 months and make those hundreds of approaches. Think how good it will feel to have all that experience under your belt. This could be an exercise for those who wish. Sit back, relax, and really visualize the future you, more confident, able to approach women with ease, thanking the present you for sticking to it and making approach after approach. Feel the gratitude and happiness. Enjoy that feeling. When you are making your approaches, re-visit that feeling of future success. It is going to happen, and you are making it happen.

> **Assignment # 13**
> Visualize the future you thanking the present you for practicing approaches and finding success. Feel the confidence that success brings.

This process really works. You have nothing to lose but loneliness and unhappiness. What you have to gain is the ability to live your life with confidence, knowing you can meet women anywhere, anytime. Go for it. You have the skills you need right now. Hone them through practice, and learn to enjoy the process. Learn and continue. Build and grow. Your efforts will pay off.

Closing

Working on the approach is just the beginning. At some point the conversation needs to lead somewhere. For our purposes there are two possibilities. Either you make plans to get together later, or you go somewhere together immediately for an "instant date." You're going to have to use your own judgment on what direction to take things. If she has to get to work, or class, or wherever, obviously the instant date is not an option. But if the vibe is right and you know someplace nearby that you can go, hop to it.

Um, don't literally hop. It's an expression. I suggest walking.

We'll explore both types of close and how to do them as smoothly as possible. Closing is not complicated, but it can be a little nerve wracking. You've spent some time building attraction and now you're testing how good a job you did. You're taking things to the next level. It has to be done right or you'll end up taking a step back in the process.

Making plans

You've been talking anywhere from 5 to 20 minutes, maybe a little longer. You admired a trait unique to her, used kino, made a Statement of Intent, continued the conversation and the kino. You are confident and interested. All systems are go.

Then she glances at her watch and says, "you know, I'm enjoying our conversation, but I really have to go." Don't blow this. The next step is really simple. There are a million ways to do it. Here is one. You say,

"I'm enjoying our conversation too, I'd like to continue it some time. When would be a good time for us to get together?"

Or, let's say her friends are calling her, and she says, "well, I've gotta run." You can say,

"That's cool. Hey, if we're both free later this week, we should hang out."

See how easy that was? Note that you are not asking for her phone number or email address, but it's natural at this point to fish out a scrap of paper and a pen for her to write these down as you figure out when and where to meet. If she just says, "I don't know," suggest something simple. "How about we have lunch, when are you free?" Or, "I'd like to show you my favorite bar, what's a good night?" There are so many ways to do this right, you really don't need to worry. Just make sure you keep your suggestions open enough that she can fill in the details. Don't say, "I know, let's meet at 3:35 on Monday at the top of the Empire State Building," especially if you don't live in New York. If your plan is too specific, she's more likely to have a reason to say no, and you're more likely to misinterpret this as her way of saying she's not interested. Make it something open like, "let's get together after work for a drink, what day is good for you?"

Got it? Sure you do. But we're going over it again anyway to make sure you really have it down. She has to leave. Or you have to leave. You say,

"I'm having a great time, I really like talking with you. We should get together for drinks sometime, what's a good day for you?"

That's pretty non-threatening, and pretty much guaranteed to get a positive response. When she says, "how about Thursday?" you say, "Great, what time?" Get out your paper and pen, hand them to her and say, I'll call you Thursday." Notice you are not saying, "please right down your phone number." You don't need to. By saying you'll call her, she knows to write down her number. While she's doing that you can say, "put your email address on there too." She will.

You've already done the hard work before you reach this point, it should feel natural and go smoothly. And it will. But you need to practice it. Sit in front of a mirror with a pen and piece of paper in your pocket. Practice making plans to get together. Keep practicing till you have it down. You're going to do great, don't worry.

Assignment # 15
Practice making plans, and getting her phone number and email address. Make it smooth and confident. Let it flow.

Instant date

This one is even easier, but only if you've practiced it. The conversation has gone for anywhere from 10 minutes to half an hour. You're tired of just standing there in the bookstore, or wherever you happen to be.

It's time for an instant date. You can say something like,

"You know, I'm having a great time talking to you. There's a cafe upstairs. Let's go grab a coffee." And off you go. Obviously, it helps if you know of a place nearby to go. A cafe or restaurant will make more sense if you're meeting her in the daytime. If you meet her at night and there's a bar nearby, that might work too. You have to read the vibe correctly and take things a step at a time. And be creative. If there's a zoo nearby, ask her if she wants to go visit the petting zoo with you. If there's a fountain, ask if she wants to go toss coins in the fountain for good luck. Let your fun side out.

Remember, I am not giving you rules or scripts. I'm giving you ideas to work from and make your own. When the instant date is over, go back to the section before this one on making plans. Depending on what you did on the instant date, you could make plans for something that takes things to the next level. If you went for coffee, the next meeting could be dinner or a bar. Don't push things to far too fast, but try to notch it up a little if it feels right. If it doesn't, then just make plans to do something low key. If she needs more time to get to know you, that's fine. Keep her comfortable and everything will go better.

Approach. Talk. Find the emotion, feeling, or trait. Notice, admire, and relate. Build attraction. Amp it up with kino, Statement of Intent, confidence and interest. When things are on a high note, move to an instant date. When it ends, or if she has to leave during the conversation and can't do an instant date, make plans to get together again. Give her a vague plan that she can flesh out. Let her choose the day and time. Give her paper and pen and tell her you'll call her.

When she's writing her phone number, ask for her email address too. Practice all of this in your mind, or in front of a mirror. Practice it in real life. Practice practice practice, and enjoy every moment. It's all part of the adventure. Let your attitude reflect that, and you will be amazed at your success.

Kiss the girl

One big sticking point for many men is knowing when it's time for the first kiss. I guarantee you if you sweat and fret about this the whole time you're with her, it will never be the right time. You need to stay focused on building a connection and attraction with her. When the moment comes in the interaction when you're thinking to yourself, "I wonder if now is the right time to kiss her," it probably is. One way to test that theory without diving in is to lean in close to her, look into her eyes and say, "I'm trying so hard not to kiss you right now." If she jumps up and runs away screaming, you did not build enough attraction yet. If she stays put, don't kiss her just yet. Let the tension build first. If you do this right, she might be the one who kisses you first.

Another approach to this is to say to her, "you look like you want to kiss me," and see how she reacts. You're not saying that you necessarily want to kiss her, just that she looks like she wants to kiss you. If she says, "What, I don't know what you're talking about," you can say, "hey, relax, I didn't say I was going to let you, I just said you look like you want to." Say this in a fun way, not a mean way. If you don't know the difference, this technique is not for you.

And then, there are those times when you just know the moment is right. Lean in closer. Maybe whisper something in her ear like, "your hair smells so good." You could kiss her ear, or her neck. See how she reacts and play it from there. And always remember, taking two steps forward, one step back is a good way to keep things at a slow, non-threatening pace.

One last kissing technique that is great if you're just ending the first meeting with her and you've made plans to meet with her again. You can say, "well, I'll see you on Thursday. Till then, here's a kiss to remember me by." Lean in and either give her a peck on the cheek or on the lips, depending on what feels right in that moment.

And keep in mind, you should have been doing kino before you get to this point. If you haven't touched her yet, the kiss is going to be awkward. The more kino you've done, the more ready she'll be for the kiss, and the more natural it will seem. Her reactions to your touch will have given you the cues you need to gauge whether she's interested in you. If every time you touch her she pulls away, it's obviously not time for a kiss. You need to go back to building a connection and building attraction.

I keep saying this and I'll keep saying it. These are all steps in a process. You cannot just read straight through this book, walk outside, and suddenly have women running to you. You need to add one piece of the puzzle, then another, then another, and practice each till you understand them and can do them with confidence. This is a building process. Don't try to learn it all at once. Do the exercises, step by step. Keep building and improving. Work on this at least a little bit every single day. If you do, success is guaranteed.

Keeping the ball rolling

Things are going better than you ever imagined. Not only are you comfortable approaching beautiful women and talking to them, you are finding all your social interactions are easier and more enjoyable. You're becoming one of those social people you always half admired and half hated. You are connecting with people in a way you didn't know was possible. When you get invited to a social event, instead of dreading it you look forward to it. One more chance to practice your amazing new skills. So now what?

Let's stay focused and keep improving. I'll assume at this point you've met at least one woman that you really clicked with and have plans to get together with her. The old you would have been calling her every second to make sure the plan is still on. The new you realizes that even if the plan falls apart, that's ok, because you are meeting interesting women all the time. You've gone from a scarcity mindset to an abundance mindset, and it shows in your confidence.

Still, it would be nice if you followed through on your plans and got together. So lets look at some tips for keeping the ball rolling. At this point, you're going to continue everything you've learned till now, but there are some special situations we need to address.

Talking on the phone

You have plans to get together, and you have her number. The day before your next meeting, you call her up. There are two possibilities, either she answers or you have to leave a message. If you leave a message, you could say something like, "Hi (her name), this is (your name), I'm looking forward to getting together tomorrow at (wherever you're going to meet). I'll see you there." That's it. If she needs to cancel she's got your number on caller ID, but don't mention that. You don't want to give her the idea you want her to cancel.

If she answers the phone, great. Don't expect to be back in the vibe immediately. You might have to open all over again, but it will be easier this time since you've already built up rapport. Don't talk too long, but try to end on a high, like right after she laughs at something funny you said. Stay relaxed and just chitchat, then say you're looking forward to seeing her tomorrow.

Like I said, this is much easier than the original approach. You already know a little bit about her, and can think of things to talk about more easily. Stay calm and confident and the phone call will go fine. If you already have concrete plans, you can skip this step. But if that means you'll be even more panicky the next day waiting for her to arrive, then make the call.

Flirting through email and texting

If you have her email address you can send her an email. If you have her cell phone number, you could text her. Either way, I would approach it the same way as the phone call until the first meeting. Keep it light and breezy.

But after the first meeting, you can use email and texting as a great way to flirt with her between phone calls and meetings. There is a different dynamic to email and text messages, it feels more anonymous, so you can get away with a more flirty tone. Ease into it and see if she responds. If not, back off and continue with the light and breezy approach. But if she does, this is a great way to get into some very sexual topics in a fun and non-threatening way. Just don't expect her to be the same way on the phone or in person. Think of each medium as a way of exploring a different side of her personality.

The next meeting

So it's finally the day you planned to get together. By the way, you've probably noticed I don't call it a date. You shouldn't either. The word "date" is too loaded with luggage and negative connotations for so many people. Just hearing the word can raise your blood pressure. You are not going on a date. You are getting together. You are meeting. No big deal. It's what humans do.

So anyway, it's the day of your get together. Let's say you're meeting for dinner. Hopefully you picked someplace low key, comfortable and fun, not stuffy, intimidating, and expensive. You get there on time and she's not there yet. Should you:

    A. Panic
    B. Start sweating profusely
    C. Run out the door screaming

D. All of the above

Choose wisely.

Ok, time is up, the correct answer is E. None of the above. Hey, no fair, that wasn't one of the choices. Well, if you've been meditating every day, you should be enlightened enough to know that sometimes you have to think outside the box. Just one more benefit of meditating. Remember the old monk who carried the woman across the stream? You thought that was just a story about not attaching, but it was also a story about not getting stuck in a rut, allowing yourself to live in the moment and act with compassion in that moment. Be flexible.

I'm really getting off track here. Ok, you're on time, she's late. What do you do? Come on, Zen boy. Picture yourself at the restaurant. It's filled with people. Maybe there's even a bar. Maybe there's a cute hostess. Maybe there's a table full of interesting women. If there's anyone who still hasn't figured out the answer raise your hand.

Yes, you talk to people. You can talk to women, men, couples, whoever you want. Why? Two reasons. First, it will keep you from sitting there stewing and worrying and sweating because you'll be too busy having fun. Second, when she finally does walk in, instead of seeing you slumped over your fifth margarita she'll see you being lively and fun and social. She might even have to go steal you away from a group of women. Hey, let them all fight over you.

Remember your abundance mindset. Even if she never shows up at all, you should still be able to have a great time. Then when she calls to apologize later, you can honestly tell her, "I was sorry you didn't make it, but I ended up having a great time anyway. Should we make plans for another time?"

Is the light bulb clicking on yet? Here is what happened. You are now Superman. You can walk into any situation and have a good time. You do not rely on any specific woman for you to feel good, confident, happy, and, well . . . super. You know that you have the super power to meet women everywhere. That is a very great power. Use it responsibly. And have fun.

Why venue change is stressful

A weird thing happens when you get together the first few times with someone new. Each time, you feel like whatever progress you made the last time has been cut in half if not more. You take a giant step back in rapport and have to start building it up again. Why is that? Well, there are lots of reasons. For one, people are not cartoon characters, they are people, subject to moods, emotions, and all manner of change. So the next time you see her, she's not the same her you saw last time. Also, assuming you are getting together in a different place, that alone is enough to change the dynamic. Whatever you do, don't let this throw you. I bring it up so you are prepared for it. It's all part of the process.

So do you go back to square one? Sometimes, sadly, yes. But even if you feel like you're just meeting for the first time, that feeling will go away much more quickly than it did on the actual first time. You'll make faster progress, regain lost ground, and be back feeling comfortable again in no time.

Think about a good friend that moves away or travels abroad, so you don't see them for months. Then they call up out of the blue, announcing they've returned. You get together and, there are a few moments of awkwardness. It's just a human thing. Get used to it, and realize that feeling passes and things go back to normal.

This can actually be used to your advantage. How? By doing a change of venue while you're with her. Say you start at the coffee place, then go for a walk outside, then stop somewhere for lunch, then go to the beach. It's like you've gone on four different dates. Every time you take her to a new place, it will just build more comfort and a stronger bond. You'll feel like you've known each other longer and have a history together. This helps you relax and be yourselves around each other. Cool, huh?

The *next* next meeting

Make sure that whenever one meeting ends, you are making plans for the next one. This avoids all manner of problems later on. You've built rapport, now is the time to bridge to the next meeting. Don't wait for a phone call later in the week, when you'll have to start from scratch before you get around to making plans. One way to do this and escalate things at the same time is to say, "Hey, if we're both free next weekend, maybe we should get together." Make the plans, then say, "That's gonna be a lot of fun. Till then, I'll give you a kiss to remember me by." Judging by her reaction, this could be a peck on the cheek, a kiss on the lips, or tongue gymnastics.

When you do get together the next time, there is no need to amp things up in terms of activities. In other words, if you ate at a greasy diner last time, you don't have to go to "Chez Expenseev" tonight. The best activities are things you just happen to be doing anyway, so there isn't so much pressure. So, if you're going to the local car dump to look for a part you need on your '78 Pinto, invite her to come with you. If you're taking your dog to run around on the beach, ask if she wants to join you. I'm not suggesting you invite her to join you for every boring moment of your life. What I am suggesting is that you don't need to do traditional "date" activities. Maybe you're going shopping at a really cool Asian supermarket you heard about, or plan on going to a book reading at a local bookstore. Whatever it is, it can be turned into a fun activity to be shared. Don't get stuck in the restaurant, movie, bar rut. There are other things to do that will be more fun and less pressure.

Hey, this is easy!

At this point, it's tempting to coast a little. Don't do it. Keep being a good listener. Keep relating to what she's saying. Keep building rapport. You are building something special every time you're with her. This never ends. If that sounds like work, see how it feels when you're actually doing it. With the right woman, you'll want to keep relating, you'll want to know her better and better. It should be fun, but you should be putting your creative energy into it every time you're together. Things will fizzle if you start taking her for granted. You need to keep this thing alive and growing, and that takes energy. But it's worth the effort. The more you put in, the more you'll get out. You could sit on your couch eating Hohos and watching TV, or you could be meeting the woman of your dreams and growing closer to her. Your choice.

Zen and the art of making love

For all you guys that flipped to this section first, get back to chapter one. You have to earn admittance to this chapter. It's easy to sit and think about sex, but that time will be better spent if you're already seeing a woman that's attracted to you.

Ok, those guys are gone, now we can talk. We're not going to get into explicit detailed instructions here. I'm guessing you understand the basic mechanics behind sex. Rather, we're going to sketch out some broader ideas that will improve whatever it is you're doing with that wonderful woman.

Focus on her

Remember how your conversational skills improved when you started listening to her instead of the babbling voice in your own head? Same principal applies here. If you focus on her enjoyment, it will be a better experience for both of you. That means you don't finish before she does. And until she does, your focus should be on getting her there. Notice what she likes and what she doesn't. Every woman is different. Don't expect her to like the same things your last girlfriend did. When in doubt, you can even ask her, "do you like this?" Yes, that is actually allowed. Just don't do it every five seconds. Usually you can tell by her reaction what she likes.

Make sex a meditation. Don't get lost in your own mind, focus on the feelings and sensations that are happening in each moment. Really get into what you taste, touch, hear, smell, and see. Let it all happen and flow. Try to relax, and try to help her relax.

Don't rush her. Let her set the pace. Don't make her feel like you are waiting for her to finish. Enjoy everything about her. Enjoy making her happy. Then you'll both be happy.

Talking about . . . um . . . you know

If you talk with her about sex, don't joke around about it in a silly way. That makes her think you're not comfortable with the subject, and that's not the impression you want to get across. You should be comfortable talking with her about sex, and if you aren't, then fake it. Gender equality is a great thing, but when it comes to sex, men are still generally dominant. Many women will expect you to make all the moves. If you got into an airplane and the pilot was joking about crashing on take off, you might want to turn right around and get off the plane. That's why every pilot on every flight you've ever been on has the exact same breezy "been there done that no big deal" sound in his or her voice. If the passengers feel like the pilot knows what he's doing, they will relax and have a better flight.

So you don't have to be deathly serious, but you do have to seem comfortable with the subject. If you ask her to tell you her fantasy, and she does, that's not a good time to turn it into a joke. It is a good time to use those listening and relating skills you've built up.

Roadblocks, hurdles, and potholes

Sometimes things are moving in a sexual direction, but then falter. She pulls back, cools off, or shuts down, and you're left wondering what you did wrong. Women get lots of weird and conflicting messages about sex their whole lives, and that can result in very mixed feelings when things heat up. Sometimes the two steps forward, one step back approach is a good idea. Let things heat up, then cool down, then heat up a little more, then cool down. If she seems suddenly reluctant, you be the one to say, "we should stop." Let her feel comfortable with the fact that this is not a matter of life and death for you. Yes, it actually does feel that way to you, but don't let *her* feel that. Let her know that she's safe.

She needs to know that if at any point she wants things to stop, they will stop. Moving things forward, then back a little, then forward more, then back a little will give her the space she needs to know she has a say in what is going on. So you could be kissing, then go back to talking a little, then back to kissing, but then your hands start exploring, then maybe back to just kissing.

Once again, every woman is different. You need to tune in to her mood to get your timing right, and that isn't always going to be easy. Err on the side of going too slow rather than too fast, and you'll avoid a lot of problems down the road.

Basking in the afterglow

When you're done with your record-breaking love fest, don't forget to stay close and focus on her. Many men feel like jumping up and wandering off after it's all over, but I don't recommend acting on that impulse unless you want your first time with her to also be your last. Actually, this would be a good time to talk about something you'd like to do with her sometime soon. I'm not suggesting you try to make specific plans since she probably doesn't have her calendar handy, but you could say something like, "you know, I really like being with you and doing things with you. We should go see a band one of these nights." This let's her know that you like spending time with her, and you're not just interested in sex. That probably sets you apart from the vast majority of men she's known. This also sets things up for later when you want to make specific plans. If you bring up going to see a band, or whatever vague plan you mentioned, it will bring back the feelings of closeness you shared the last time you mentioned it.

Wow, that's cool stuff. The main thing I want you to remember is to pay attention to her and what she enjoys. Make sure she's having a good time if you want to be this close with her again. Make it a good experience for her, and don't rush things. Let her feel comfortable and relaxed, and it will all go much smoother.

Oh yeah, and use a condom, cowboy.

Relationships - making them last

You've done all the assignments. You've met a ton of great women. Things are going great. Your friends all consider you a master pickup artist and have started asking you for advice on how to meet women. Life is good. And then, out of the corner of your eye, you see her. Everything slows down. The music sounds different. There are sparkles in the air. She notices you and your eyes lock. A little baby with wings floats by and shoots an arrow in your heart. And you think two things. First, why doesn't that baby have a diaper, and second, I think I'm in love.

Ok, it doesn't really happen like that, but don't tell anyone in Hollywood. What really happens is you start seeing more of someone, and find out you really feel great when you're with her. She's got that something special that no one else had. So after a while you're seeing more of each other. And more and more. After a few months you're calling her your girlfriend. After a few more months you're moving your cats into her apartment. Now all the friends that were looking up to you are giving you concerned looks.

Try as we might, sooner or later most of us realize that we cannot lead the life of a bachelor forever. Notable exceptions include Hugh Hefner, but I think it's safe to say that Hugh is not reading this book. He's got his hands full with women already, if you know what I mean. For most of the rest of us, a long-term relationship is inevitable, so the question then becomes, how do you make them last.

Everything we've discussed up to this point, everything we've practiced, is all part of what will make the relationship successful. Being a good listener, relating to her on an emotional level, showing appreciation for who she is as a person, and staying alive and aware, awake to every moment, these are the things that will help you grow with her. Being your own person within the context of the relationship is always a challenge, but that challenge is like any other you have faced to this point. Meeting the challenge allows you to grow in new ways, so that you can fulfill potentials you never realized you had. Ideally, you will bring out positive qualities in her, and she in you, that would otherwise have lain dormant.

Bad relationships are often bad because each person is trying to impose their own values and sense of self on the other. Good relationships involve nurturing the things you appreciate in the other person, rather than chastising and nagging about the things you don't like. Communicating, listening, relating, and staying open to change and growth will make the relationship healthier and more enjoyable. And remember, if she tells you about a problem she's having, don't jump into problem solver mode. Have empathy for her, listen and relate. Being there for her means being aware of her feelings, not trying to solve every problem she encounters. This includes times when the problem is you. If she complains about something you did, she might be looking for you to acknowledge that you weren't paying attention to her feelings, rather than you saying some specific way to avoid that specific problem in the future. Be aware that she might be using a specific example to point out a broader issue. Yes, sometimes it seems like women are speaking in code, but if you follow the advice in this book you will break the code. You will be listening not just to her words, but to the feelings and emotions behind those words. Learn this one trick, and your interactions with most women will go smoother. And your relationships too.

Not that it's all going to be smooth sailing. It's not. But that's where daily meditation gives you an advantage. Having that time each day to remove yourself from a tight focus on the crisis of the moment, and to open to a broader context and dwell in that sense of being, that is what helps you to gain insight and see new ways of resolving conflicts.

Not all relationships will be a success, but it's possible to transition from lovers to friends rather than going from lovers to haters. The closeness you've built up with the other person doesn't have to be thrown away. If instead of "breaking up" you are just changing the intensity and nature of the relationship, it can mean less pain for everyone. That might sound like I'm just playing with words or making euphemisms, but in practice it really is possible for an intimate relationship to end without the underlying relationship ending or turning negative.

For those relationships that just keep going and growing, always keep in mind those things that drew you to her and her to you in the first place, and keep those things alive. The world can be a nasty place at times, it's nice to know there's someone on your side. Be that person.

Remember, you're coming from an abundance mindset. You chose her because she's special, not out of neediness. There are a lot of great women out there, but she had that extra something special. Let her feel that.

Indra's Net

One important realization that comes with meditation is the interconnectedness of all beings and things. One metaphor Buddhist's use to explain this connectedness is called Indra's Net. The universe is like a net with a jewel at each vertex, the place where the ropes intersect. Each jewel is reflected in every other jewel, and each jewel in turn reflects all other jewels. This is similar to the concept of a hologram, where every part contains the whole.

We all truly are interconnected. If I yell at Frank, then Frank feels bad and has an argument with Sally, and she takes it out on Bill, and so on. It spreads out like the ripples on a pond. Likewise, if I show compassion to Frank, this will spread out in positive waves. Every action has a reaction. Every cause has an effect. Put simply, what comes around goes around.

When you see a woman from afar, it's easy to delude yourself into thinking that you are two separate and distinct beings. But through continued meditation you can slowly strip away this conditioned way of thinking and misinterpreting the world. You can see the true interconnectedness of all beings. You and she are already connected, but you must help each other peel away the layers of delusion to reach that place of being connected, now, in this one and only moment. I hope that this book has shown you a path to realizing that connectedness, and that you can share that realization with others in your own way. We are each of us a jewel on Indra's net, reflecting each other, infinitely connected and interconnected. We are each waves on a vast ocean. Dive into that ocean and see what you find.

Final words

I wish you luck with all your romantic endeavors, and with all of your life. I hope you practice the ideas in this book and make permanent positive changes in your life. In particular, I hope you meet lots of women and learn how to relate to them on a deeper level, so that when you meet the one with that extra something special, you know what to do to make things work with her. You deserve to be happy, and so does she. Live your life, and let it all happen, together.

Good luck on your journey.

Additional Reading

Hey, we've covered a lot of territory here, but if you want to go deeper, there are lots of great books about Zen out there. Here's a list of some that I've particularly enjoyed:

Hardcore Zen: Punk Rock, Monster Movies, & the Truth about Reality, by Brad Warner

The Three Pillars of Zen: Teaching, Practice, and Enlightenment, by Philip Kapleau Roshi

Zen Mind, Beginner's Mind, by Shunryu Suzuki

The Compass of Zen, by Seung Sahn

Nothing Special: Living Zen, by Charlotte J. Beck

Not Always So: Practicing the True Spirit of Zen, by Shunryu Suzuki

At Hell's Gate: A Soldier's Journey from War to Peace, by Claude Anshin Thomas

4074028

Made in the USA
Lexington, KY
18 December 2009